Listening to God

A practical and biblical guide
to recognizing God's voice

David Théry

English version 2021

Éditions École de Ministère Surnaturel Francophone

Email: contact@ecolemsf.com

The biblical quotations used are taken from the English Standard Version.

Cover design and illustrations by Alain Auderset

Cover design: Émilie Charette and Samuel Béland

Legal Deposit - Bibliothèque nationale de France 2021

ISBN: 9782956581970

Printed in Poland. www.arkadruk.pl

ENDORSEMENTS

"Listening to God" by Pastor David Théry is one of the most inspiring and practical books I know on the theme of prayer and the voice of God. Imbued with the presence of God, this book will activate your spiritual sensitivity and propel you into a new season where you too can hear the voice of the Holy Spirit without a doubt.

MICHAËL LEBEAU,

President and Co-founder of EMCI TV

The one who listens to God, to the Spirit of His Word, is steadfast in his ways, she or he is led and leads others into the rich and glorious inheritance of the Kingdom of Heaven. David Thery is a man who seeks the depth of God in simplicity of application, you will enjoy this book!

MICHEL BISAILLON,

Superintendent of the Quebec District of the Pentecostal Assemblies of Canada

You have most certainly made the following reflection: "But how can I hear God speaking to me? "Hearing God's voice is definitely what every Christian yearns for in her or his heart of hearts. Throughout my life and in the ministry that God has entrusted to me, hearing the sound of his voice is one of the most beautiful melodies I have ever heard. It was his voice that inspired me to start the evangelism site ConnaitreDieu.com which has impacted millions of people around the world in more than 25 languages. It was His voice that inspired me to start the daily email A miracle every day that today helps hundreds of thousands of people in their daily walk with

Jesus. It was His voice that reassured me when I was faced with the greatest challenges in my life or ministry. I believe that God speaks and that he also yearns to be heard by His children. This is the invitation that my friend, Pastor David Théry, offers us in this book, proposing to live the listening of God as a true spiritual experience, one that traces the way to the heart of the Father. We learn how to interact with God in a new, fresh and transforming dimension. At the end of this process, there is the joy in feeling loved by the Father, the joy of hearing Him and being closer to him. Throughout the pages of this book, you will develop an ever-growing hunger for intimacy with God. In this sense, this book grows the spiritual appetite. It reveals the heart and open-mindedness of the author who gives us an approach to intimacy with God in a practical, deep and striking way. Also, it is a joy for me to recommend this book to those who long to be like the apostle John, known as the one who was close to Jesus. My prayer is that through its pages and by the grace of God, readers will be enriched by this truth of God's word in John 10:27: "My sheep listen to My voice, I know them, and they follow Me. »

ÉRIC CÉLÉRIER

Founder of TopChrétien, author of Divine Connections

To me, this book is a demonstration of David's pastoral heart. Indeed, he longs for each of us to listen to God's Spirit with active faith, and he urges us in that direction so that our lives would better reflect the intervention of God's Kingdom on earth.

PAUL TÉTREAULT

Assistant to the Superintendent of the Quebec District of the Pentecostal Assemblies of Canada

The supernatural is an increasingly neglected dimension within the contemporary church while God is still acting in a powerful way all over the world. David Théry is literally an ambassador of the Holy Spirit and through this book, you will find faith in miracles and especially the desire to be a tool in God's hands to live in a new dimension of the supernatural. David is an extraordinary advocate of the subject. He knows how to make practical the lifestyle where miracles are daily and within everyone's reach. I recommend reading this book to all those who thirst for more and want to learn how to live more with God.

LUC DUMONT

songwriter, singer, coach & speaker

Finally a beautiful book on how to hear the voice of God and walk with the Holy Spirit written in French by a French speaker. I am so grateful for my friend David Théry who is a leader in the Spirit movement and an example of living in intimacy with God. His work reflects his gift as a teacher and his ability to popularize biblical principles so simply that it moves us, touches us and challenges us to want more from God. To all those who thirst for God, who long to hear His voice, obey Him and be mightily used by Him, this book is for you! By putting into practice the shared tools, words of wisdom and biblical truths taught in this book, you will enter the dimension that every believer longs for: to hear the voice of our Heavenly Father and to see God at work through you. So get ready! In a few pages, your life won't be the same!

JOËL DUMAINE

Founder of the Generation:Unity movement

My friend Pastor David Théry is a remarkable man of God. Like a gold digger in the Wild West, he set out to hear God. David is an outstanding teacher and I have been privileged to benefit from his teaching on listening to God. This book is a very practical manual for anyone who wants to develop an intimate relationship with their Lord and enjoy a rich and abundant life in Him. Thank you David for who you are and for your incredible ministry! May the Holy Spirit continue to use you for church building!

SERGE HERRBRECH

President of the Union of Protestant Assemblies on Mission

ACKNOWLEDGMENTS

This book is a condensed summary of my spiritual journey over the last five years. Life with God, though personal, is enriched by the life that flows from the members of the body of Christ.

First of all, I am grateful for Sylvie, my wife. You are more prophetic than I am and you are an inspiration to me. Thank you for your perseverance in following God no matter the cost is. Thank you for your love and patience, thank you for being my wife and a wonderful mother to our daughters. Thank you for the team we make. Thank you for re-reading this book. I love you.

Louise Dunn, thank you for showing me the ministry life like Jesus: doing only what God shows you. Thank you for your prayers and friendship. You are precious in our lives.

Thank you Lysa, Marjorie and Bruno you are a wonderful team, without you I could not have devoted myself to writing this book. You walk in listening to God and I know that your future is glorious, I already miss you.

I am extremely grateful to Paul and Denise Goulet. I have experienced a real transformation through your ministry, you are role models.

My journey listening to God has accelerated through contacts with my friends, Jean-Frédéric Laroche and Benoit Therrien. Thank you!

Joël and Hannah Dumaine, thank you for working at the revival in Quebec and making it spill over into the French-speaking world.

Éric Célérier, Nathalie Almont, thank you for trusting me for the training entitled" Hear the voice of God "on TopFormations.

Jérémy and Anabelle Sourdril, Michael and Yveline Lebeau and the Enseignemoi team! You are making a real difference by bringing God's presence into every Christian home! Thank you!

Crossroads of Nations, thank you for your thirst for God and your trust in my experiences, for the prayer and encouragement.

Thanks to the team of correctors: Philippe Théry, Daniel Niambi Batiotila, Marceline Ouedraogo, Sylvie Théry.

Holy Spirit, thank you for your friendship and patience with me in my learning.

FORWARD

Slow down the pace to hear His voice

This book by Pastor David Théry will help you (as a song that I particularly enjoy says) to "slow down the pace". In this world where there are many voices, you will be encouraged to listen to the voice of the good shepherd and discover His love.

Sometimes we have to step aside from other voices to listen only to His, and sometimes we even have to silence our voice to hear well. Relax, calm down, stay still, take the time to listen to it.

A friend was encouraging me recently, saying, "Your Father has a lot to tell you. "I believe this is true for you as well.

It would be a shame to read at full speed and absorb this book without putting it into practice. That's why it's important to slow down and take the time to act on His Word.

Too often, God speaks and we are not aware. It is so important to know how to listen to and remember God's words, just like Mary who kept in her heart all that the shepherds told her about Jesus.

Too often, believers have their ears open to lies and satanic accusations. It is time to open our ears wide to the divine call.

He who is alive will speak to you. He will strengthen you, make you strong, make you unshakeable.

I received this word for you:

And the king made silver and gold as common in Jerusalem as stone, and he made cedar as plentiful as the sycamore of the Shephelah.

(2 Chronicles 1:15).

In the same way, His words will become to you as common as the heaven above your head, for the earth will be filled with the knowledge of the LORD, as the waters cover the bottom of the seas. Drink from His water whenever you are thirsty! In His love,

JÉRÉMY SOURDRIL

Co-founder of Enseignemoi.com, author of the bestsellers: 365 days in the heart of the world, Unfair love, 365 days in the heart of proverbs and 365 days at the feet of the master.

TABLE OF CONTENT

INTRODUCTION

Have you ever wanted to hear God speak to you after reading the life of a biblical character, hearing a speaker preach about his or her intimacy with the Lord, or reading a book of testimonies?

These experiences are not reserved for an elite or sovereignly chosen officials. You too can hear God speak to you. For two simple reasons: the first is that God is alive and speaking. The second is that He has a plan for you, but He does not give you a detailed map in advance. You must follow His voice to enter into your destiny. To follow God's guidance is to live by faith. Every child of God is called to live by faith, which is to listen to Him.

This simple principle seems to get complicated when you want to put it into practice. How can we hear God? How do we recognize his voice? What to do with what he tells us? How do we develop better listening skills? What are the biblical bases for listening to God?

This book is not a theological teaching to satisfy your intelligence. It is a practical and biblical guide to listening to God, experiencing the life of the Spirit and becoming an effective ambassador for the kingdom of God. By applying this teaching, your spiritual life will take off, your perception of God will change, your fellowship with Him will intensify, the fruit your life bears will multiply. Each chapter is followed by practical exercises. I encourage you to do them seriously, it is not the content of this book that will transform you, but its practical application, because you will be interacting with God on a whole new level. This is the beginning of a great adventure! Don't be afraid, fasten your seatbelt, we are taking off!

I asked the Lord what he wanted to tell you for each of these chapters. Then I explained biblically what I had received, illustrating it with testimonies.

This is what I have received from God for you by listening to him.

Jesus' letter to you

I am close to your heart. Don't be afraid, I want to quench your thirst. I put my Spirit in you so that I can speak directly to your heart. You must believe that my Spirit is in you and that I want to talk to you. Be silent and wait for me, I long for you.

I speak to your mind, your intelligence must submit to it. Learn to recognize my voice so that you can follow me. And so that you will not follow the enemy. I want to lead you by my Spirit.

Don't be discouraged. You don't learn a language in one day. You will make mistakes, that's normal, but I will reward your efforts. You are not alone, I am here to guide you. Rely on my Word. I am waiting for you.

I want to open your eyes to show you what I do. My Spirit reveals to you, it shows you spiritual realities. Accept what I show you. Expect to see what I will show you. Let yourself be led by me.

It is I who created you. I can touch every part of your being. When two people are in communion, they exchange, laugh or experience emotions together and also communicate physically. I love to hold my children in my arms. Receive my affection.

My Spirit is always with you. When you sleep, your mind is more receptive because your thoughts are at rest. Expect me and don't let what I communicate to you fall to the ground. I draw you closer to me. The dreams I give you pass through the obstacles that prevent you from listening to me when you are awake. I am close to you when you sleep like a mother who watches over her sleeping child and whispers words of love.

I am God, I know everything and I demonstrate my love and power, my care for each of my children. Draw from my knowledge to open hearts. I have the key to every door, to every heart. I want to reveal mysteries and secrets in my intimacy.

Do not drop my words on the ground. Take time to examine what you receive, hold on to what is good and hold it in your heart, lean on my words to move forward. My words are food for your soul, do not let the bread I give you be stolen. You will need to meditate on what I am telling you so that your thoughts will be changed. Keep them preciously as love letters.

I long to commune with you. It is this communion, this friendship that I seek. Do not be afraid of me. I am here for each one of you, you have my full attention. Come closer to learn more. As a little child asks questions to her or his parents, don't be embarrassed. You won't always get the answer you want, but I will guide you with love.

I have come so that you may be free, completely free. Free from what you are not aware of, but which holds you captive. I am the liberator. The more you listen to me, the less power and influence the enemy will have in your lives. Renounce to lies and embrace the truths I reveal to you through my Spirit. I want to lead you to peaceful waters and green pastures.

I have put my Spirit in you to guide you, to destroy the works of the devil and establish my kingdom. By working with me, you will see my will being fulfilled. What is important is not what you can do, but what I will do when you will obey me by faith. Do not be afraid, I am with you.

The source that I have put in you must spring up and flow on those around you so that they may taste my love, so that my life may pass through you. My words through you will produce life in hearts, give courage to my children. Go forth humbly by faith and observe the fruit.

RRARR
NO DROG NO PROB
BUM B
PITIPITIPITI!

YES, HILOO?
WHO'S IT?

WHHAATT? GO...GOD?!
CRAZY! I CAN'T BELIEVE IT!

HE... HE WANTS YOU TO CALL HIM BACK!
©A.AUDERSET

PRAYER

CHAPTER 1.

GOD WANTS TO SPEAK TO YOU

On the last day of the feast, the great day, Jesus stood up and cried out, "If anyone thirsts, let him come to me and drink. Whoever believes in me, as the Scripture has said, Out of his heart rivers of living water will flow'" Now this he said about the Spirit, whom those who believed in him were to receive, for as yet the Spirit had not been given, because Jesus was not yet glorified.

John 7.37-39

These are the things I received from the Lord as I listened to him in preparing this first chapter:

I am close to your heart. Don't be afraid, I want to quench your thirst. I put my Spirit in you so that I can speak directly to your heart. You must believe that my Spirit is in you and that I want to talk to you. Be silent and wait for me. I long for you.

God is close to your heart

People often think that God is far away, in the clouds, but nothing could be further from reality. When someone is born again, the Holy Spirit comes to dwell within him. This is a reality.

But he who is joined to the Lord becomes one spirit with him.
1 Corinthians 6:17

We understand from this verse that there is a union in spirit between our spirit and God's Spirit, the Holy Spirit. This intimate union allows God to speak to us from within. Christians often remark, «I felt inside me that I had to talk to this person,» or «A little voice inside me was telling me to do this. «That little voice is actually the voice of the Holy Spirit. God is so close to us that we can easily confuse His thoughts with our own. I often hear those who want to learn to hear God say, «I thought it was my imagination. «Stop waiting for a voice like thunder to be heard through the broken clouds! God will speak to you in the intimacy of your heart and your thoughts, for He lives in you. The fact that He uses our language may seem hard to believe, because it sounds too simple! Instead, read this testimony from an Internet user who attended the «Hearing the Voice of God» training on TopChrétien:

For the first time I really heard God's voice, so simply. I hear Him speaking to my heart through my thoughts and I am slowly learning to recognize His voice, it is such a liberation that it is so simple!

Don't be afraid of Him

Fear is a common reaction to the manifest presence of God. But if we allow it to paralyze us, we will deprive ourselves of what God wants to give us freely.

When the Hebrews came out of Egypt, the Lord led them to Mount Sinai. He then let them hear His voice, like a trumpet sound, from the top of the burning mountain, and Moses began a dialogue with God (Ex 19:16-19). However, the people were so afraid of God that they said to Moses, «We are going to die! Listen to God and then tell us what he said. «(Exodus 20:18-20). Here we see that the Hebrews refused God's invitation to come into His presence and hear His voice. When Moses went up the mountain, not only did he not die, but when he came down, his face shone with the glory of God. One can be afraid of God because of the misconceptions one has about Him. For example, we may think that He will punish us, that He is angry or that we will disturb Him, or that we don't deserve to be near Him. All these conceptions are lies. The truth is that God is good, that He loves us and wants to be in communion with us. That is why He has come to make His home in us, to be close to us! So don't be afraid to talk to Him!

Another common form of fear is the fear of the Holy Spirit. Since spiritual experiences are beyond the control of reason, there is a form of apprehension about the Holy Spirit. But Jesus reassured us about this. Let us read the following verse:

What father among you, if his son asks for a fish, will instead of a fish give him a serpent; or if he asks for an egg, will give him a scorpion? If you then, who are evil, know how to give good gifts to your children, how much more will the heavenly Father give the Holy Spirit to those who ask him!"

Luke 11.11-13

If we ask the Father for what we need, that is, to hear His voice, to receive the words that come out of his mouth to nourish us (Mt 4:4), he will give us good things, the Holy Spirit.

So, although I don't control what the Lord is going to tell me, although I don't grasp all the mysteries of God in me, I shouldn't be afraid. The Holy Spirit will not hurt me like a scorpion or a snake, the Holy Spirit will feed me with the words of God like some good bread.

God wants to quench your thirst, but are you thirsty?

If anyone thirsts, let him come to me and drink.

John 7:37

Jesus explains very clearly that the most important criterion for God to quench our thirst, even before coming to him, is our thirst. The last verses of the Bible are addressed to the thirsty people:

The Spirit and the Bride say, "Come." And let the one who hears say, "Come." And let the one who is thirsty come; let the one who desires take the water of life without price.

Revelation 22:17

Jesus does not give any other condition, because He has already paid everything, everything accomplished at the cross. There is no restriction on your level of holiness, your maturity, your understanding, the only condition for receiving the rivers of life from the Holy Spirit is to be thirsty and to come to Jesus. God loves us so much and respects us so much that He does not force us to drink. Some torture practices consist in making people drink to death. God does not want to torture us, so Jesus speaks to those who are thirsty.

The second good news of Jesus's invitation is that there is no limit to thirst. We can drink as much as we want, even to the point of becoming a source for others, we will talk about that later. This water that Jesus gives quenches our thirst, fills us, quenches our thirst.

The first time I listened to God speak to me, I felt like someone in the desert, licking condensation off a bottle of fresh water and had just discovered how to drink the water inside to quench his thirst. The first thing the Lord said to me was, «David, I love you, I've been looking forward to this moment. «I was overwhelmed by these words, I felt filled with God's presence like never before. What a memorable day! Since then, I have drunk from the source of the Holy Spirit within me, my soul is quenched, safe, and at peace. The river of living water that Jesus speaks of is a water that gives life and peace, communicates God's love, it is the river of God and it never dries up.

God has put His Spirit in you to speak directly to your heart.

Or do you not know that your body is a temple of the Holy Spirit within you, whom you have from God?

(1 Corinthians 6:19)

God has placed His Spirit in us, the Holy Spirit. The Holy Spirit speaks, but since He speaks within us, inside us, the big question is: how can we recognize Him among our thoughts? Even before we can distinguish our thoughts from God's thoughts, it is important to recognize, accept, and expect Him to speak to us.

Listening to God's voice is not forcing God to speak, but learning to listen to Him. God spoke to you before you believed in Him, and He drew you to Him in this way. Since He has lived in you, He has continued to communicate with you, but you may not always have listened to Him. When we talk to someone who doesn't listen to us, we tend to stop talking to them or wait for them to talk to us. It's a bit like that with the Holy Spirit. He is a person, not just a spiritual force. You have to expect him to speak to you, and recognize His voice. For example, you can respond to him by saying, «Thank you, Holy Spirit, for your guidance, thank you, Holy Spirit, for your comfort. By engaging in dialogue with him, you will receive more of his thoughts. I advise you to say this simple prayer now:

Thank you, Jesus, for giving me the Holy Spirit. Holy Spirit, I acknowledge that you live in me and I ask your forgiveness for all the times that I did not pay attention to your voice, for the times that I opposed you. I decide to listen to you, talk to me and teach me to recognize your voice in me. In the name of Jesus, Amen.

You have to believe that He is inside you and that He wants to talk to you.

Whoever believes in me, as the Scripture said, out of his heart rivers of living water will flow (other translations: from his heart, from his inner being, from his womb).

(John 7:38)

Jesus mentions in this verse that we must believe in Him. Faith manifests itself when we want to listen to God. In truth, we will hear a voice within us that resembles our thoughts, feel things, have impressions or see images in our thoughts and we will have to believe that it can come from God.

Your faith must be based on the fact that God lives in you and that he wants to talk to you. That being said, faith is taking a risk. Believing that God speaks to me is taking the risk of believing that it is He who speaks to me, taking the risk of believing what He says, to do what He tells me.

Notice that Jesus mentions the location of the source. This source is within us. What unleashes the flow of God's words within us is to believe that He is there and wants to speak to us. This is what Jesus calls drinking. Drinking is to receive the water flowing in us, receiving, welcoming God's thoughts through faith. It is not about creating the source, or producing thoughts, but simply recognizing what is already present in us.

Be silent and expect Him

O LORD, in the morning you hear my voice; in the morning I prepare a sacrifice for you and watch. (other translations: I watch, I wait).

(Psalms 5:3)

Have you ever met someone who talks non-stop, asks questions and gives the answers herself or himself? It then becomes difficult to express one's point of view in the presence of this kind of person. This is in that same way that many Christians pray and talk to God, but do not let him speak. The first rule of dialogue is that one must be silent in order to listen to the other speaking. Often, believers talk to God, but because they do not expect Him to answer them (thinking He is far away or too busy or they doubt that God will hear them), they do not take the time to listen to Him. When we expect God to speak to us, we wait before him in silence. Silence is difficult for many, our world is so hectic. Moments of silence are rare. Yet the psalmist here shows us how he approaches the Lord. He stands before Him and waits. When was the last time you waited in silence before God? This waiting that the psalmist speaks of here is a state of focusing on God («I turn to You»), but also an attitude of faith. In fact, the verb «to wait» can also be translated as «I watch» or «I'm watching». It can evoke the attitude of a hunter waiting for a prey to pass in front of him, or a sentinel watching a guard post. It is not a matter of killing time, but of expecting something from God.

If when you turn to God in silence, you begin to think about what you have to do, your to-do list for the day, just write it down on a piece of paper to keep your mind free and then keep waiting. A good exercise is to take your watch and say to God, «Here I am Lord, I am turning to you and expecting you, what do you want to tell me today? «Then stand in silence before the Lord for a full five minutes, then write down what you have experienced, felt, or thought about.

God longs for you

But when you pray, go into your room and shut the door and pray to your Father who is in secret.

(Matthew 6.6)

Most religious exercises serve to attract God's attention, but few people can believe that they already have His attention. Our Heavenly Father wants to commune with us. He gave Jesus so that we might be reconciled with Him and be set free from sin. More than that, he adopted us, he made us his children. His care for us is such that he knows everything about us and is waiting for us in our room. God is already there, waiting for us, he wants to talk to us.

When we understand that God yearns to talk with us, we enter into His presence and rest and can simply receive His words. It is like someone who wants to listen to a radio station. His desire to listen or his efforts to turn on his receiver and tune the right frequency have no effect on the transmitting station. The station broadcasts the program whether people listen to it or not. To listen to it, all you need to do is create the conditions for a good reception and start listening.

There is a real reward in listening to God

God will deposit in your heart thoughts that will resemble yours, but will produce fruit in you, unlike your own thoughts that cannot do so. Indeed, when God speaks, His word is Spirit and life, it produces what it declares. For example, when God says, «Let there be light! «the light was. When Jesus said, «Peace be with you! «we feel His peace and our anxiety fades away. Likewise, when God comes to encourage Gideon, He begins to change the way he perceives himself and ends up accomplishing feats.

Taking the time to listen to God has produced many changes in my life. First of all, I have developed greater inner security. The Lord has often told me, «I am here with you. «So I came to believe Him, and my thoughts were renewed, and then my actions and reactions changed. God has also revealed to me-and he continues to do so-how much He loves me. There is a big difference between intellectually accepting that God loves me and receiving and living His love. Everybody needs to feel loved, to hear Him say it. When God affirms it in our hearts, his love saturates our whole being to the point of overflowing and spilling over onto those around us.

The apostle Paul wrote, «If God is for us, who will be against us? «(Rom 8:31). I sang it, declared it, but it became a reality when God spoke to me about how proud he was of me. I didn't expect it. One morning I asked him what he wanted to tell me, and like a bolt of lightning the thought came into my mind: «David, I am proud of you! «At that moment, I said to myself that those must be my thoughts, that it was pride. But this thought persisted in me. I realized that many biblical texts support the fact that God takes pleasure in us, that He rejoices to see us walking in his ways.

> *The LORD your God is in your midst, a mighty one who will save; he will rejoice over you with gladness; he will quiet you by his love; he will exult over you with loud singing.*
>
> *(Zephaniah 3:17)*

Often, under appearances of humility, we believe lies that paralyze us. I realized that I simply had difficulties believing with my heart that the Lord was taking pleasure in me, which affected the way I saw myself. This was also the case with Gideon 1. God had a plan of victory for him, but he saw himself as less than nothing.

If all the heroes of God who are hiding from the enemy heard God declare their true identity to them, the kingdom of darkness would quickly be destroyed. You don't have to wait for the angel of the LORD to come and speak to you, God has put His Spirit in you for this purpose! By listening to God within you, you will enter into your destiny, transformed by God's declarations of your identity.

Daddy, look at me!

When I take my daughters to the park, I hear them shouting every thirty seconds: «Daddy, look at me! « every time they climb on a new game. Everyone needs to know that their daddy is watching. Likewise, the approval and the benevolent gaze of our heavenly Father is very precious. Sadly, sometimes the children of God become fully engaged in activism to draw the Lord's attention to them. Conversely, when we experience a true dialogue with God, His presence becomes more tangible in our lives and peace is established, we no longer act to be seen and we serve God because we are loved and assured of His attention.

Now it's time to listen!

On the last day of the feast, the great day, Jesus stood up and cried out, "If anyone thirsts, let him come to me and drink. Whoever believes in me, as the Scripture has said, out of his heart will flow rivers of living water.'" Now this he said about the Spirit, whom those who believed in him were to receive, for as yet the Spirit had not been given, because Jesus was not yet glorified.

(John 7.37-39)

In the next chapters we will in more detail learn how to recognize God's voice, but since you are a child of God and He lives in you, you should be able to hear Him within you without further explanation. Here are four tips for hearing God's voice within you:

- Be calm before the Lord.
- Focus on Jesus.
- Welcome, and drink the spontaneous thoughts/ images that come up inside you.
- Write down what you receive as you go along for later review.

Calm yourself before God

But when you pray, go into your room and shut the door and pray to your Father who is in secret. And your Father who sees in secret will reward you.

(Matthew 6.6)

To have a conversation with God, you need to cut yourself off from distractions. Remember that the Lord will speak in you, since He lives in you. You will need to concentrate to recognize His gentle voice; calming yourself down will help you concentrate more easily. It is possible to be in a quiet room and not be quiet inside. Take time to confide your burdens to Jesus and praise Him for entering into His presence. If you can think of things to do, write them down to take care of them after your appointment with your heavenly Father. Some people are able to calm down quickly, for others it takes practice. Do not be discouraged. Listening to soft, inspiring, wordless music will help you. This is what the prophet Elisha did.

But now bring me a musician." And when the musician played, the hand of the LORD came upon him.

(2 Kings 3.15)

Focus on Jesus

Jesus said, «He who is thirsty, let him come to me. «Since we want to hear from God, we must come to Him. By focusing on him, you are listening. Remember that young Samuel received this advice from Eli when God was calling him:

Therefore, Eli said to Samuel, "Go, lie down, and if he calls you, you shall say, 'Speak, LORD, for your servant hears.'" So, Samuel went and lay down in his place.

(1 Samuel 3.9)

Speaking to God and expecting to hear Him is an act of faith. It is this simple faith that releases the river of living water within us. Jesus said, «Whoever believes in me, rivers of living water will flow from his bosom. »

So you can simply ask God what he wants to tell you or ask Him a question, then quiet down and wait for His answer while you stay focused on Him.

Drink from God's river

Jesus affirms that we can drink from this spring that gushes forth within us. We can expect to receive spontaneous thoughts or images, like a gush within us. Drinking is a way of saying that we are to welcome, to receive that which rises within us.

These thoughts can be elusive or insistent, the images can be vague or very detailed; stay focused on Jesus and receive what springs up in you.

Write down what you receive as you go along for later review.

Do you have to believe that everything you think about comes from God? No, of course not, but we have seen that God will speak in you, because He lives in you, so writing down what you receive is the first step to drinking from the river. When we receive something from the Lord, we tend to reason or analyze what He tells us as we go along. This legitimate reaction causes us to stop listening. The same thing happens when you listen to someone while thinking about what you are going to say to them. You may not understand everything the person has shared with you. True active listening consists in giving 100% of your attention to the person you are listening to. So by faith, be attentive to what comes up in you (thought or image) and simply write it down. We will see in the next chapter how to distinguish what comes from God from what comes from our own thoughts.

Testimonials of first listening

One day while I was teaching on this subject at a Bible school, a student had a vision, he saw an eye. He drew it and then asked God why he was showing it to him. God said, «You are precious to me as the apple of my eye. « This young man was completely overwhelmed by the love of God that came over him as a result of this revelation. Let us remember that this image is very biblical, it is in this way that God protects his people, as the following verse indicates:

But the LORD'S portion is his people, Jacob his allotted heritage. He found him in a desert land, and in the howling waste of the wilderness; he encircled him, he cared for him, he kept him as the apple of his eye.

(Deuteronomy 32:9-10)

Another of these students also had a vision. He saw himself on a cliff and in front of him stood the globe. The Earth was formless, the continents were not drawn. When he asked God what this meant, the Lord answered, «Before the Earth was created, I was already thinking of you and loving you. «This student began to cry unrestrainedly, so saturated was this simple word with God's love that his heart could not contain it. Let us remember that this word the student received is very biblical:

Even as he chose us in him before the foundation of the world, that we should be holy and blameless before him.

(Ephesians 1.4)

A similar experience occurred for the wife of a pastor who was attending a teaching session on «Hearing the Voice of God". I suggested that the listeners begin listening to God by asking if He loved them. After a few seconds, the woman began to cry. When the listening time was over, each person shared what they had received. This pastor's wife was actually overwhelmed by the words of love that God had imprinted on her heart. She confessed that she knew what the Bible said about this, but she doubted God's personal love for her. Her heart was filled with peace and joy following this confirmation in the intimacy of her heart.

Do you want the Lord to reveal His love personally to you too? I suggest that you say this prayer aloud:

Jesus, here I am before you, I believe that you live in me by your Spirit, I thirst for your living waters. Here I am Lord, speak, your child is listening. Reveal to me how much you love me, speak to my heart.

Let me pray for you now:

Lord, I pray for the person reading this prayer. May his or her spiritual eyes be opened so that he or she may have visions. May his or her spiritual ears be opened so that he or she can hear your voice clearly within. May your love spring forth in her heart and create a deep intimacy with you, Father. In the name of Jesus, Amen.

Practice exercise

Now it's time to put into practice what you've just read! Relax physically and mentally and take notes. I advise you to start a prayer journal by taking a notebook or writing on your computer. Play some instrumental music, for example by clicking on this link :

entdi.eu/piano

Focus your attention on Jesus and then say:

«Lord, here I am, speak, your child is listening. »

Focus on the Holy Spirit within you and write the following question:

«Lord, how do you love me? »

Stay focused on Jesus in you and then write down what comes spontaneously into your mind (thought, image). Do not try to analyze while you are receiving.

Remain in simple faith, just like a child, while you receive. Once you are finished (give yourself time, at least ten minutes), review what you have received.

- What has this produced in you?
- Does the Bible support what you have received?

So beautiful here...
It's too bad one can't see God... It would be much easier to believe in him

If at least one could hear him

Well, it's true!
?
Why couldn't he just talk to us?

Sorry, what d'ye say??
Plop!
Plop!
?!
A.Auderset © www.auderset.com

?!!
I think, I've just got it!

CHAPTER 2.

RECOGNIZING HIS VOICE

My sheep hear my voice, and I know them, and they follow me.
(John 10.27)

But he who enters by the door is the shepherd of the sheep. To him the gatekeeper opens. The sheep hear his voice, and he calls his own sheep by name and leads them out. When he has brought out all his own, he goes before them, and the sheep follow him, for they know his voice. A stranger they will not follow, but they will flee from him, for they do not know the voice of strangers.
(John 10.2-5)

These are the things I received from the Lord as I listened to him in preparing this chapter:

I speak to your mind, your intelligence must submit to it. Learn to recognize my voice so that you can follow me. So you will not follow the enemy. I want to lead you by my Spirit.

God speaks to your spirit, your mind must submit to it.

The sheep recognize that they need to follow the shepherd, for if they go alone, according to their own thoughts, they will get lost. Jesus used this comparison because we, too, must accept to be led by the Holy Spirit. From the time you were born, your intelligence and reasoning have directed your life. When you were born again, the Holy Spirit came to revive your spirit that had died because of the sinful nature you had inherited from your parents. So it is your spirit now that is in fellowship with the Holy Spirit.

But he who is joined to the Lord becomes one spirit with him.
(1 Corinthians 6:17)

The fact that your spirit is connected with the Holy Spirit allows you to live in fellowship with him, but as with any relationship, this connection must be developed and maintained. Your mind, if not subject to your spirit, can stifle this relationship with the Holy Spirit. On the contrary, the more you stimulate your mind, the more you can enjoy fellowship with the Holy Spirit. This is important because the Christian life is spiritual, a constant interaction with the spiritual world through our spirit.

For if I pray in a tongue, my spirit prays but my mind is unfruitful.
(1 Corinthians 14:14)

The apostle Paul distinguished between the spirit and the intellect. This verse shows us that my mind and my spirit are two different things, but above all that they are independent.

It is possible to pray with the mind but without the spirit participating and in the same way, it is possible to pray with the spirit without the mind intervening. What does this mean?

Our intelligence conceives things through reasoning, logic, it is based on experience. Our mind is in relationship with the Holy Spirit and receives from Him directives, inspirations, impressions, visions, concepts, thoughts or revelations. While I can understand the reasoning of my mind, I must receive by faith what my spirit receives from the Holy Spirit.

My intelligence can even oppose my mind, and this for several reasons. First of all, the flesh (of which intelligence is a part) opposes the spirit and its desires are contrary to it, as explained in the following verses:

> *But I say, walk by the Spirit, and you will not gratify the desires of the flesh. For the desires of the flesh are against the Spirit, and the desires of the Spirit are against the flesh, for these are opposed to each other, to keep you from doing the things you want to do.*
> *(Galatians 5:16-17)*

But even when one decides to live by the spirit and no longer live according to the flesh, one cannot always logically understand the things of the spirit. Our intelligence can censor our mind. Surely it has happened to you before when you have thought: «It must be my imagination, it's just a dream, it doesn't make sense, it's not logical, it's not possible, etc.». »

This is where faith comes in. Faith leads our intelligence to submit to our spirit and thus to the Holy Spirit. Here is a biblical example to illustrate this important truth. Ananias was a disciple of Jesus. He was in prayer when the Lord told him to go to Saul of Tarsus and pray that he would regain his sight and receive the Holy Spirit. God even gave him the address!

> *Now there was a disciple at Damascus named Ananias. The Lord said to him in a vision, "Ananias." And he said, "Here I am, Lord." And the Lord said to him, "Rise and go to the street called Straight, and at the house of Judas look for a man of Tarsus named Saul, for behold, he is praying, and he has seen in a vision a man named Ananias come in and lay his hands on him so that he might regain his sight." But Ananias answered, "Lord, I have heard from many about this man, how much evil he has done to your saints at Jerusalem. And here he has authority from the chief priests to bind all who call on your name." But the Lord said to him, "Go, for he is a chosen instrument of mine to carry my name before the Gentiles and kings and the children of Israel. For I will show him how much he must suffer for the sake of my name." So, Ananias departed and entered the house. And laying his hands on him he said, "Brother Saul, the Lord Jesus who appeared to you on the road by which you came has sent me so that you may regain your sight and be filled with the Holy Spirit." And immediately something like scales fell from his eyes, and he regained his sight. Then he rose and was baptized; and taking food, he was strengthened. For some days he was with the disciples at Damascus.*
>
> *(Acts of the Apostles 9:10-19)*

It was the spirit of Ananias, who was in communion with the Holy Spirit, that enabled him to receive Jesus' guidance in a vision. His mind argued and opposed what his spirit had just received. Saul was a killer of Christians and had the power to put Ananias in prison. Ananias did not want to die! If Saul had gone blind, it seemed to be good news for the believers in Damascus. If so, why restore his sight? How was it possible that Saul could be praying to Jesus, who was chasing the Lord's disciples? How could we intellectually accept that Saul had a vision of Ananias coming to lay hands on him? Where is the logic in Saul's call to proclaim the Gospel? There is no logic! The intellect cannot grasp God's plan. Jesus reassured Ananias because his questions were legitimate, but Ananias still had to follow his spirit instead of his intelligence.

> *For my thoughts are not your thoughts, neither are your ways my ways, declares the LORD. For as the heavens are higher than the earth, so are my ways higher than your ways and my thoughts than your thoughts.*
>
> *(Isaiah 55:8-9)*

God's thoughts are different from ours. It is necessary to lean on our faith to receive them. When we listen to God, we must expect him to convey things that are beyond us.

It is then that Ananias decides, by faith, not to follow his intelligence, but his spirit and thus obey Jesus to go and pray for Saul. Because Ananias listened to Jesus in his mind and did not let his intelligence censor what he received, he obeyed God. What was the result? Saul regained his sight and received the Holy Spirit through Ananias' prayer.

Put yourself in Ananias' shoes, what would have been your reaction? If you want to hear God and obey Him, you must submit your intelligence to your mind, develop your spirit. Hearing the voice of God is a spiritual experience, it is your mind that will receive the thoughts, visions and impressions, not your intelligence.

God knows how to convince you that it is he who is speaking to you; once the demonstration is made, it is up to you to decide to believe him. Here's what one person experienced on this subject:

I am completely surprised! I thought I would not be able to hear the voice of God. Not only do I hear Him, but I find Him both loving and humorous. Especially in his requests for prayers for the most unlikely of people! Since I am a young Christian, sometimes I doubt, and my prayer is then for asking God to tell me if it is really him who is speaking to me, and somehow to give me a strong sign? The strongest having been Latin words... which could absolutely not have come from me! With of course a very strong message! There is no longer any doubt, that it is just me speaking to myself, it is undeniably God. It is a formidable formation that strengthens the bond with our heavenly Father. God is supernatural! Extraordinary!

You too can move from doubt and ignorance, to wonder and joy in being in communion with God.

Let us pray together:

Lord Jesus, I decide today to submit my mind to my spirit and to accept by faith your thoughts and visions. I renounce trying to understand everything intellectually and I accept that you lead me. I expect to receive your thoughts that are superior to mine. In the name of Jesus, Amen.

Learn to recognize the voice of God

When he has brought out all his own, he goes before them, and the sheep follow him, for they know his voice.

(John 10.4)

I proposed my wife Sylvie to marry me almost 22 years ago. I know her voice, I can identify her in the middle of a crowd, on the phone, or in the dark. I have learned to recognize her and her expressions and intonations. I can also discern my wife's emotions just by listening to her. The reason for this ability is the time we spent together. Jesus says that his sheep know his voice. In the same way, spending time listening to God allows us to recognize His voice. It is a learning experience. We will discuss this notion of learning in the next chapter.

At this point, I want to immediately undo the lie that claims that there are Christians who hear God and others who are incapable of doing so. A shepherd leads His flock at the sound of His voice. All the sheep of Jesus are called to recognize His voice and follow him.

For all who are led by the Spirit of God are sons of God.
(Romans 8:14)

Just because something is available to everyone does not mean that everyone is living it. Thus, God wants all men to be saved, but not all are saved. Ignorance can deprive us of what is available. That is why we are studying together how to recognize God's voice.

Let us pray together:

Lord Jesus, I believe that you are my shepherd, I am your sheep and I believe that you want to lead me at the sound of your voice. I decide to learn to recognize your voice in order to follow you and not to follow the enemy. In the name of Jesus, Amen.

Why is it necessary to learn to recognize God's thoughts? To avoid following the enemy! Indeed, there are many sources of thoughts within us. Everyone has an inner language, we talk to ourselves, we think. These thoughts are the fruit of your reasoning, an association of ideas or memories. They can also come from circumstances, such as a conversation with a person for example. Since your thoughts are very present inside you, which is normal, you must learn to put your intelligence at rest. This will allow you to perceive God's thoughts in your mind. A good way to put your mind at rest is to speak in tongues softly before listening to the Lord.

For if I pray in a tongue, my spirit prays but my mind is unfruitful. (1 Corinthians 14:14)

Once your mind is at rest and you ask God questions, expect to receive His answers in the form of spontaneous thoughts or images that will rise up within you. This factor of spontaneity is important because it will show that these thoughts are not the fruit of your reasoning.

If you turn on your TV, a picture appears without you being able to anticipate it. The spontaneous appearance shows that it is not your imagination, but does not guarantee that it is the program you wanted to watch. You must therefore consider other factors.

If someone is pretending to be Sylvie on the phone, I will be able to recognize the deception by evaluating certain characteristics of the voice I hear. First, the tone of voice and the intimacy. Because I spend time with her, I am used to the sound of her voice. Our intimacy makes her call me by a nickname that she is the only one to use. In the same way, as you learn, you will recognize the mark or signature of God's thoughts towards you.

If it is God who is the source of a spontaneous thought or image, then what He says will reflect His character and nature. God is love, so it is normal that God's thoughts are filled with love for us. God is patient, encouraging, compassionate, kind, joyful. God forgives, He saves, He is truth. When God speaks, he cannot say things that are contrary to His nature. For example, if you receive a thought like this: «Come to me to be forgiven, trust me,» it sounds like the character and nature of God revealed in the Bible. Indeed, the Lord draws us to Him (John 6:44), He is faithful to forgive us (1 John 1:9), and it is through faith that we receive His grace (Eph 2:8).

The more you read the Bible, the more you will be able to assess whether a thought can be of God, because you will be able to analyze it according to your biblical understanding of God's nature.

Your intelligence may oppose God's goodness if you have low self-esteem. If you think you are worthless and God tells you during your listening time that you are precious, you must realize that this is also what the Bible says about you and that you are believing a lie about your worth if you hold on to the thought of being worthless. You may find it hard to believe that God loves you so much, that He believes in you so much, that He is so patient with you. But if you are experiencing this inner struggle, you must decide to submit your mind to your spirit, believe what the Bible says, and reject the lie.

Jesus calls you by your first name

God is a personal being, He speaks in the first person. You can therefore receive thoughts by which God expresses Himself in this way. Jesus says that he calls His sheep by their name so He can call you by your first name. This experience usually produces a sense of wonder, because it allows us to realize how well the Lord knows us personally. Let us remember how Jesus spoke to Mary in the garden of the tomb:

> *Jesus said to her, "Mary." She turned and said to him in Aramaic, "Rabboni!" (which means Teacher).*
>
> *(John 20.16)*

When Jesus rose from the dead, he called Mary by her first name when she thought she was talking to the gardener. It was then that she recognized the Lord and answered him: «Rabbouni,» which is a respectful form of «Rabbi,» which means «Master. Jesus shows His affection for us by calling us by our first name. This produces in us, in return, a surge of affection towards Him. You may hear your name in you as the Holy Spirit calls you. Don't resist it, just answer, «Yes, Holy Spirit, I am listening. »

The Holy Spirit speaks softly

> *And he said, "Go out and stand on the mount before the LORD." And behold, the LORD passed by, and a great and strong wind tore the mountains and broke in pieces the rocks before the LORD, but the LORD was not in the wind. And after the wind an earthquake, but the LORD was not in the earthquake. And after the earthquake a fire, but the LORD was not in the fire. And after the fire the sound of a low whisper.*
>
> *(1 Kings 19.11-12)*

When we want God to speak to us, we often expect to live a very intense experience, to hear an audible voice, something indisputable. Yet the Lord simply presents Himself to us, He speaks within us. God's thoughts are often sweet and light and can be easily interrupted by our own thoughts. There are many reasons for this. First of all, in a relationship of intimacy and fellowship, we should not need to shout to talk to each other or to get each other's attention. God can call out to you with a wink, a smile, a hand on your shoulder. Secondly, it is written that the righteous will live by faith. God speaks to us clearly enough to make us believe it is He, but it is our faith that must be in action, and faith is about taking risks. By taking the risk of believing that the Lord is speaking to me, I am demonstrating my faith, which is what pleases Him most.

> *And without faith it is impossible to please him, for whoever would draw near to God must believe that he exists and that he rewards those who seek him.*
>
> *(Hebrews 11:6)*

Silence is an act of worship

God does not control us, we are free to listen to Him and follow Him. By speaking softly, God invites us to listen to Him calmly and to be calmly before Him, which is a form of humility and dependence. If I want to hear Him, I must stop and put him before my activities and concerns.

> *"Be still, and know that I am God. I will be exalted among the nations, I will be exalted in the earth!"*
>
> *(Psalm 46:10)*

By listening to Him, in the quietness, I honor him as God. That is why silence is a form of worship. In silence I am at rest, I have nothing to produce. I can then discern His voice within me and receive visions. As I was writing this paragraph, I took a time of silence before God. After a few minutes, I began to physically feel His presence on my face and then the Lord gave me two visions while I closed my eyes.

The first was a wick in a perfume diffuser. I would see the wick first soak in the perfume and then come out saturated to diffuse it. When the wick became drier, it went back to the bottom of the diffuser to saturate again. Then I saw an oil lamp wick. The wick was burning, but it didn't burn. The Lord then made me understand that by remaining in His presence in silence, one is like this wick that saturates itself with the kingdom of God and is then able to diffuse it. We must immerse ourselves in His presence. The wick of the oil lamp means that serving the Lord must not consume or destroy us. The source of God's fire in our lives must be our intimate relationship with Him. Then Jesus said to me, «Teach my children to stand in silence before me. «I believe with all my heart that God will reveal Himself mightily to you if you learn to stand in silence before Him.

God loves your company

God loves our company. By speaking softly, we come closer to Him to hear him better and He likes it!

After saying these things, Jesus was troubled in his spirit, and testified, "Truly, truly, I say to you, one of you will betray me." The disciples looked at one another, uncertain of whom he spoke. One of his disciples, whom Jesus loved, was reclining at table at Jesus' side, so Simon Peter motioned to him to ask Jesus of whom he was speaking. So that disciple, leaning back against Jesus, said to him, "Lord, who is it?" Jesus answered, "It is he to whom I will give this morsel of bread when I have dipped it." So when he had dipped the morsel, he gave it to Judas, the son of Simon Iscariot. Then after he had taken the morsel, Satan entered into him. Jesus said to him, "What you are going to do, do quickly." Now no one at the table knew why he said this to him. Some thought that, because Judas had the moneybag, Jesus was telling him, "Buy what we need for the feast," or that he should give something to the poor.

(John 13.21-29)

John was close to Jesus and their friendship was manifested in an intimacy that the other disciples did not have. John could whisper in Jesus' ear and hear the secrets he gently revealed to him. The apostle is the author of the Gospels who gives the most space to the words of the master at His last supper. It is normal, he was right next to Jesus. When Peter motioned to John to ask Jesus who would be the one to betray Him, Jesus just answered John. The Lord spoke to him so softly that the other guests did not hear his answer. Only John had the revelation that Judas would deliver Jesus. So the other disciples did not understand Judas' departure, because they had not heard the words of the Lord. God loves our company and He whispers His secrets to His friends, those who stand in silence before Him.

The Holy Spirit knows how to speak to you

A basic rule of communication is that the person who expresses himself or herself must try to make himself or herself understood by the other person. The thoughts of God in us are communicated to us for a purpose, we must be able to understand and receive them. If God spoke to us in a foreign language, we would not understand what He wanted to tell us. If he used images whose meaning is impossible to grasp, they would have no effect on us. That is why God usually uses our language, words and images that we understand. In the same way, each Bible writer was inspired by the Holy Spirit, but he used his own vocabulary. So expect God's thoughts to be like your thoughts.

If, for example, you are a mechanic enthusiast, chances are that God is using metaphors and comparisons related to this field to speak to you. Don't reject them, don't neglect them. They are not your thoughts, it is just God speaking your language to touch your heart.

Sometimes what God is showing us is not immediately obvious at first glance.

Recently, I was teaching on «Hearing the Voice of God» at the French-speaking School of Supernatural Ministry . During a time of listening, a young woman received a vision of a field of red tulips when she simply asked the Lord if He loved her. She picked up her phone and googled the symbolism of red tulips. The answer was «eternal love." At the same time, her husband, sitting next to her, heard God say to her, «I love you with an everlasting love. «What a beautiful confirmation! Both spouses had tears in their eyes, touched by this demonstration of love from their heavenly Father.

God speaks and communicates His life

A major difference between our thoughts and those of God is the effect produced in us. When God speaks, our hearts respond differently because God's word is creative and life-giving. If, for example, I try to encourage myself and stay positive about a situation, the effect of my thoughts is limited and ephemeral. On the other hand, if the Lord comes to encourage me, it is not just information that I receive, I also receive courage, but a lasting, supernatural courage that is beyond understanding. This is why the Apostle Paul had written to Timothy to fight by relying on the basis of the prophetic words he had received. The word of God communicates life. You will therefore find that God's thoughts provoke a particular reaction in you: excitement, conviction, faith, life, wonder, peace, fear of God (a deep reverence for His person), or joy, strength or courage, consolation or comfort. To use a comparison, our personal thoughts and ideas would be like reading a restaurant menu. We can salivate, imagine the dish, but without tasting it. God's thoughts, on the other hand, would be eating the dishes mentioned on the menu. With every bite (every word), we experience a wide range of sensations (smell, texture, taste, satiation).

Not to follow the enemy, listen to God!

Now the serpent was more crafty than any other beast of the field that the LORD God had made. He said to the woman, "Did God actually say, 'You shall not eat of any tree in the garden'?" And the woman said to the serpent, "We may eat of the fruit of the trees in the garden, but God said, You shall not eat of the fruit of the tree that is in the midst of the garden, neither shall you touch it, lest you die.'" But the serpent said to the woman, "You will not surely die. For God knows that when you eat of it your eyes will be opened, and you will be like God, knowing good and evil."

(Genesis 3.1-5)

The enemy also speaks in your head. As he did with Eve, he tempts you, makes you sin, makes you disobey the Lord. These temptations often happen spontaneously, because they are not the fruit of your reasoning. Satan makes you doubt, questions what God has said with suggestions, questions, drawing you to death, one thought at a time («Did God really say?») The devil is the father of lies and he lies to you without scruples (he had the audacity to declare to Eve: «You will not die. «He tries to stimulate your pride («You will be like gods.») Satan encourages you to live a life independent of God to keep you away from His presence (remember that Adam and Eve hid from God when they heard His voice in the garden after they sinned).

Eve listened to the enemy, believed him and followed his instructions. The next thing we know, sin, death and sickness entered the world and Satan has been ruling the earth ever since. If you don't recognize the voice of God, there are probabilities that you won't recognize the voice of the enemy either. As the enemy will speak to your flesh, your mind will likely find it logical what he will propose to you. You may therefore follow the enemy regularly instead of being guided by the good shepherd, while pretending to follow God. Satan wants to destroy you, steal you and take you away from the Lord. On the contrary, Jesus wants you to have life in abundance. Who do you want to follow? Who do you want to listen to? Who have you listened to so far?

Listening to God is not an option for a particular category of Christians, it is a necessity in order not to be influenced by the enemy. As you have surely understood, we recognize the thoughts of the enemy by the fact that they are spontaneous, that they reflect his nature and bring death and destruction into our lives.

All that the Father gives me will come to me, and whoever comes to me I will never cast out.

(John 6.37)

For God did not send his Son into the world to condemn the world, but in order that the world might be saved through him.

(John 3.17)

She said, "No one, Lord." And Jesus said, "Neither do I condemn you; go, and from now on sin no more."

(John 8.11)

God does not condemn us, He does not judge us, He never rejects us when we approach Him. You must therefore refuse any thought of condemnation, rejection or judgment, because it does not come from God. Either it is your thoughts that need to be renewed by believing the Bible, or it is the enemy speaking to you and you do not want to listen to him or follow him! The thoughts of the enemy produce sadness and despair in us (that is what drives people to suicide), overwhelming, discouragement and paralysis to prevent us from entering into our destiny and accomplishing the works that God has prepared for us. The accuser sows guilt in us with deceptive thoughts and emotions. If we do not discern that it is the enemy who speaks to us, we will accept what he tells us and allow ourselves to be manipulated into finally obeying him voluntarily.

If therefore you discern that the enemy is speaking to you, tell him:

«Satan, I have recognized you, I am not listening to you, I reject these thoughts in the name of Jesus».

Let us pray together:

Father, I ask your forgiveness for all the times I have listened to the enemy instead of listening to your voice. I acknowledge that I followed him voluntarily and I decide to turn away from his plans for me. Father, increase my discernment so that he can no longer manipulate me with his lies. I choose to follow you by faith, Lord, on the path of truth. In the name of Jesus, amen.

God wants to lead you by His Spirit

For all who are led by the Spirit of God are sons of God.

(Romans 8:14)

The Lord leads us to the sound of His voice, but it is we who decide to follow Him. This is a characteristic of the children of God. Abraham did not become the father of believers because he heard God or recognized His voice, but because he obeyed by faith what God told him. The only way to make progress in listening to God is to trust and obey what God says. The more you listen to Him, in the silence of His presence, the more you will recognize His voice and that of the enemy. The more you decide to follow the guidance of the Holy Spirit, the more your faith will increase, for you will see the fruit of it. God's joy will increase in your life, and His peace and love will be more present in you. You will develop a trusting relationship with the Holy Spirit. Persevere, your spiritual faculties will grow if you use them. I want to end this chapter by praying for you.

Lord, I pray that you will stir up in your child's heart the thirst to recognize your voice. I pray for a deposit of faith so that he/she may trust you. May his/her heart be saturated with your love and may he/she be able to walk the path you have planned for him/her by following your guidance. In the name of Jesus, Amen.

Practice exercise

Now it's time to put into practice what you've just read! Relax physically and mentally and take notes. Play some instrumental music, for example by clicking on the following address:

entdi.eu/piano

Focus your attention on Jesus and then say:

«Lord, here I am, speak, your child is listening. »

Focus on the Holy Spirit within you and write the following question:

«Lord, what do you want to tell me in your voice? »

Stay focused on Jesus in you and then write down what comes spontaneously into your mind (thought, image).

Do not try to analyze while you are receiving. Remain in simple faith, like a child, while you receive. When you are finished (give yourself time, at least ten minutes), write and then examine what you have received

- ·What has this produced in you?
- ·Does the Bible support what you have received?

IF ADULTS HAD TO LEARN TO WALK

CHAPTER 3.

PERSEVERE IN ORDER TO BE REWARDED.

These are the things I received from the Lord as I listened to him in preparing this chapter:

Don't be discouraged. You don't learn a language in one day. You will make mistakes, that's normal, but I will reward your efforts. You are not alone, I am here to guide you. Rely on my word. I am waiting for you.

Don't be discouraged, you can't learn a language in one day.

The first time I heard a teaching on «Hearing God's Voice» on a podcast, I tried it for a few minutes at the end of the message. At that time, God was already speaking to me in different ways: often through verses when I was reading the Bible or through inner convictions coming from the Holy Spirit. Sometimes the Holy Spirit would even warn me by taking His peace away from me, as a way of drawing my attention to something He wanted to share with me. At this point I wanted to go further in my fellowship with God and I longed to hear His voice speak directly to my heart. However, in this first experience of listening to God's voice after hearing this podcast, it did not work well. Indeed, I was stressed, I thought to myself inwardly, «What if it doesn't work? What is God going to tell me? What if He tells me something I don't want to hear? Do I have a spiritual problem if I don't receive anything? I'm a pastor, I should hear God! »

I finally asked God this simple question: «Lord, do you love me? «After a few seconds, the silence became unbearable and I decided to stop this exercise and continue my activities. My head was filled with reasoning and anxiety. It wasn't until a year later, while I was attending a training program, that I heard a pastor talking about the benefits of listening to God. Sylvie was with me and on the way home, she took a notebook, isolated herself in the room, and after a good hour, she came to show me what she thought she had received from God. She had filled several pages and as I read them, I was moved, so moved for it was God, through these words, showing tenderness, compassion and love.

Those words written on paper were spirit and life, my heart beat faster as I read them. I then made the decision to persevere until I heard God too and it became natural. Learning to listen to God is a process that requires perseverance, like learning a foreign language. It is actually learning the language of the Holy Spirit. So, as a result of my wife's experience, I took at least ten minutes every day for more than a year to listen to God and keep a journal.

I was discouraged by the silence. It's a bit like someone who is learning a foreign language and when he or she arrives in the foreign country he or she can't say a single word because of stress. It's a sort of blocking. After a few hours or days of immersion and perseverance, this person will be able to use the rudiments of the new language. In the same way, it is important to persevere to learn the language of the Holy Spirit. Remember that God created you and lives in you. Therefore, He knows how to speak to you and how to be heard. All you have to do is learn to listen to Him.

Sylvie, on the other hand, began to hear God right away. She was receiving so much that her challenge was to distinguish her thoughts from those of God.

Her discouragement came from mistakes

Indeed, some people listen more naturally than others. When God speaks to us, we place our trust and faith in him and we take risks by doing what he tells us. When we make a mistake, we can be disappointed, discouraged or hurt. The enemy whispers to us that the best way not to be disappointed is to stop listening to God. Recognizing God's voice is a learning process. Imagine a person learning a foreign language and saying one word instead of another, or whose accent causes misunderstandings or even confrontations. If this person allows the embarrassment to overwhelm him or her, he or she will refuse to say another word for fear of embarrassment. Yet we have all learned to speak English, one word at a time. I have three young daughters and sometimes they use one word for another. Sometimes it's funny and it requires systematic repetition on our part. It's normal, you can't learn a language without making mistakes. We can master the basic rules of grammar and conjugation, but we can't think of everything when we speak! It has to become natural. It's the same thing with the Holy Spirit's language. So how do you overcome mistakes?

First of all, you must take an emotional step back. Just as a person who is learning a foreign language should be able to laugh at his mistakes, remember that the earth will not open under your feet if you mistakenly think you have received something from God. God knows that you are learning, and He is in fact very happy with your efforts and perseverance. He encourages you to continue. He will speak to you in new ways many times until you understand the message. He knows it, He is patient.

Secondly, a student who wants to gain experience in caring about people will connect with for example a host family. In the same way connect with people who are more experienced or who are also learning to hear God. You will be able to share your experiences and compare the sum of your biblical knowledge with what you receive. As it is said, there is more wisdom in two heads than in one!

Read the following testimonial!

When I was preaching in my church, I was teaching about the value we have in the eyes of God. I then asked the people in the audience to take some time to listen to what God wanted to tell them about it. After a few minutes of silence, we shared at the microphone what people had received. A fellow church member had had a vision of a chest full of gold coins and God had told him that he was more precious to him than a treasure.

This believer was moved by the intensity of this revelation. A few days later, I received an email from a woman who had listened to this teaching on our website. She, too, had listened to God. She had received the same vision of the chest full of coins, but she thought that it was pride, that it could not come from God. As she listened to the testimonies, she was encouraged, for this other beliver's testimony was a confirmation that she had indeed heard the Lord! It was an opportunity for her to cast lies on her self-esteem. Glory be to God!

Remember that Jesus is the head of his body, the more you are connected to the head, the more you should be connected to the body. It is a source of security and blessings. Third, always keep an attitude of humility.

Love never ends. As for prophecies, they will pass away; as for tongues, they will cease; as for knowledge, it will pass away. For we know in part and we prophesy in part.

(1 Corinthians 13:8-9)

The apostle Paul had received tremendous revelations directly from Jesus, but he taught that some of it is prophesied and some of it is known. This means that everything we receive is partial, each one receives a part, so the more we are in unity, the more we can add up what we receive and have a complete picture of what God wants to reveal to us.

So we persevered, Sylvie and I, and our lives were completely changed because of the new relationship we both have with the Lord. Very regularly, we receive similar or complementary things, but it also happens that we received opposite things which required us to seek confirmations. You may have your spouse as a listening companion of God or a friend who has an active spiritual life.

The more you practice, the more progress you will make.

For a long time I thought that spiritual gifts were fixed, static and innate, but the fact is that spiritual gifts and abilities develop when you use them.

His master said to him, 'Well done, good and faithful servant. You have been faithful over a little; I will set you over much. Enter into the joy of your master.'

(Matthew 25:21)

Although this verse is not directly related to hearing God, the principle remains valid. God gives more to those who are faithful with little. Do not despise small beginnings. What is important is not how many words you receive, but what it produces in you. Just as a relationship between two people is built up in stages, your intimacy with the Holy Spirit will grow stronger and stronger. Be thankful for all that the Lord communicates to you and persevere.

You will make mistakes, it's normal, but God will reward your efforts.

Do not despise prophecies, but test everything; hold fast what is good.

(1Thessalonians 5.20-21)

When we listen to God, it is like prophecy. Prophecy is listening to what God says to someone else or to a group of people.

Paul is clear, we must not despise prophecy. Why would anyone want to despise prophecy? The reason is simple: anyone who listens to God can be wrong and is learning. Therefore, if we allow the mistakes of others to affect us, we will despise the prophetic realm in general, like someone who would refuse to eat fish because he swallowed a fishbone in the past.

It is our responsibility to examine what we personally receive or what someone says they have received. Paul does not only recommend: «Examine what comes from beginners, examine if it is unusual or examine if you do not know the person. «No, the rule applies to anything we believe we have received from God. So don't be hard on yourself; you are learning and will learn all your life long. So stay tuned to what the Lord wants to tell you personally.

The apostle insists on keeping what is good, because we tend to reject everything as soon as there is an error. In other words, eat the fish and spit out the bones. This verse is encouraging beginners. Paul teaches us that we can receive good things in the midst of our mistakes. So yes, you will make mistakes and you will sometimes confuse your thoughts with those of God. But what you are going to receive from God is good , will be helpful for you and you will desire more.

Give yourself the right to make mistakes, otherwise your faith will be paralyzed.

Because you must believe by faith that God is speaking to you, your faith will lead you to take the risk of being wrong. If you don't take that risk, you will never know if it was the Lord speaking to you. When God revealed Himself to Moses in the burning bush, Moses talked with God. Put yourself in his place! He had to believe that the voice he heard in the burning bush was that of God, but above all he had to rely on that voice to go to Pharaoh, leader of the largest army in the region, and ask him to free the Hebrew people, who were the economic strength of Egypt. The Lord answered him something intellectually disturbing:

> *He said, "But I will be with you, and this shall be the sign for you, that I have sent you: when you have brought the people out of Egypt, you shall serve God on this mountain.*
>
> *(Exodus 3.12)*

So Moses had to take the risk of doing what God told him by faith. Confirmation would come once he had obeyed completely. No matter your experience, no matter your spiritual acuity, faith will always consist in taking a risk, because you will never be 100% sure that it is God speaking to you before you have obeyed.

You will therefore have to experiment in the sense of trying out, leaning in. Look at the fruit of your obedience and deduce afterwards if you had heard God.

> *And without faith it is impossible to please him, for whoever would draw near to God must believe that he exists and that he rewards those who seek him.*
>
> *(Hebrews 11:6)*

God prefers the attitude of someone who takes risks by faith, because he believes he has heard it and is wrong, to the behavior of someone who, for fear of being wrong, takes no risks. The good news is that the Lord rewards the one who seeks Him, not the one who is perfect or makes no mistakes.

So even in your mistakes, expect God, because your faith attracts His attention.

Faith intervenes in your concentration

And after the earthquake a fire, but the LORD was not in the fire. And after the fire the sound of a low whisper. And when Elijah heard it, he wrapped his face in his cloak and went out and stood at the entrance of the cave. And behold, there came a voice to him and said, "What are you doing here, Elijah?

(1 Kings 19:12-13)

If you believe that God wants to speak to you, you must decide to pay attention to what you receive. Your level of concentration will depend on your faith and therefore on your ability to take the risk of making a mistake. What is the link between faith and concentration? The Prophet Elijah decided to leave the cave when he heard a faint voice (other translations: a soft voice, a light murmur, the sound of a gentle breath, a subtle silence, a gentle breeze). According to the Larousse dictionary, tenuous means «barely perceptible». If God speaks to you in a soft murmur, you must by faith seize what you receive, take the risk of leaning on this light murmur, even if you are mistaken. The fear of being wrong may prevent you from listening. Imagine a hunter lurking in a hiding place in the forest. He hears a slight rustling of leaves. He has two options: hold his breath and listen, because he thinks it might be game, or start saying out loud, «It must just be the wind! «and drive the game away. With every sound, the experienced hunter pays attention and stops moving. It is this concentration that will eventually allow him to make a good catch. However, he will certainly have held his breath several times to hear just the wind blowing. Don't let the fear of making a mistake prevent you from grasping what God wants to share with you.

Faith comes into play when you submit your mind to what God tells you.

Your mind receives what God says, but your intelligence filters out what you decide to accept. It is possible, and it will happen often, that your mind will try to censor what the Lord tells you. There are many reasons for this censorship. The first comes from the lies you believe. God speaks according to His truth and not according to your truth. If God's truth comes up against a lie rooted in you, your intelligence will oppose it, under the pretext of defending your truth, which is in fact a lie from God's point of view. Every lie you believe is a truth to you, because no one wants to voluntarily and consciously believe lies. This conflict between your truth and God's TRUTH will manifest itself from time to time, and you will have to accept by faith that the Lord may tell you something that does not seem true to you. The key to being transformed and renewed in your thoughts is to accept and receive by faith thoughts that do not seem true to you at first glance, in order to examine them in the light of the Scriptures afterwards. If you don't take the risk of going beyond the censorship of your intelligence, you will remain captive to the lies you believe without realizing it. We will discuss this subject in more detail in Chapter Ten. Of course, when I say «that don't seem to be true,» I am not talking about things that are contrary to the Bible. Personally, when God first said to me, «David, I love you,» I couldn't believe it; my brain and heart were against it. I had been a Christian for sixteen years, a pastor for seven years, but deep down inside, without my knowing it, I doubted God's love for me. I had preached a series of messages about God's love, I could talk about it, quote Bible verses, but I had never heard God tell me personally. In fact, I had hoped that God loved me, I believed by faith that He loved me, but it was more a hope than an unshakeable conviction. So I refused to write down what I received in my mind. Three days in a row, God repeated the same thing to me. It was only on the third day that I decided to take the risk of writing what I was receiving and to silence the censorship of my intelligence. I then experienced God's love like never before. In fact, if you don't take the risk of receiving God's thoughts, you deprive yourself of what they are supposed to produce in you.

The second reason is that the Lord is going to tell you things that will surpass you, that will surprise you. You will only be able to grasp them by faith. Take Abraham, for example: although he is old, his wife is barren and has long since passed the age of having children, God speaks to him in a vision and shows him the stars.

> *And behold, the word of the LORD came to him: "This man shall not be your heir; your very own son shall be your heir." And he brought him outside and said, "Look toward heaven, and number the stars, if you are able to number them." Then he said to him, "So shall your offspring be."*
>
> *(Genesis 15:4-5)*

Faith leads us to believe God for the impossible. If the Lord tells you only reasonable, logical, predictable, and intellectually graspable things, it is because you have put Him in the box of your intellectual conceptions.

Whether it is for a miracle, a word of destiny, a prophecy, an encouragement, expect God to speak to you in a way that resembles Him.

You are not alone, God is there to guide you.

God is a personal being, not a force or energy. You don't go near a lifeless machine that refuses to answer because it doesn't have the right password. The Holy Spirit will guide and instruct you and teach you His language. It is a learning relationship. Everyone is different and the Holy Spirit knows you perfectly. He will speak to you in a way that touches you personally, tells you what you need to hear and go at your own pace. He will guide you and gradually reveal Himself to you. Don't compare yourself to others. Just as a child may have a special relationship with his father,(different from the relationship his brothers and sisters have with him) the Holy Spirit will develop a unique relationship with you. Remember that He is patient, He takes into account your ignorance, takes pleasure in your efforts, celebrates your faith, and rewards your progress. Do not focus on a method, but on the person of Jesus. You are not alone in front of a blank page, you are in the presence of your Heavenly Father who loves you and wants to talk to you.

If you ask the Lord a question and you receive nothing, don't make a big deal out of it, ask another question or start again later. My diary is strewn with unanswered questions. Remember that this teaching is to hear God better, not to make Him speak, it is not a way to force Him to speak, or an interrogation technique. God is a person, He says what He wants to say, no one can force Him. There are things that He will reveal to us in silence and others by reading his Word or by a sermon, a book, a friend, our spouse. Regularly I hear in my heart: «Read my Word» while I listen. When I then open the Bible in my ongoing reading, God begins to reveal mysteries to me and change my perspective.

You will find that the Lord speaks with varying degrees of emphasis. Remember that He is able to attract your attention if He wishes. The fact that He speaks to you less loudly or with less insistence is not a proof of distance, but a proof of intimacy. He knows that you are listening to Him; He doesn't need to shout anymore. He loves your faith and it pleases him to see you move forward following his soft voice.

Some thoughts or visions will be insistent and accompanied by physical sensations, strong emotions, even tears. Your heart cannot remain insensitive to God's love. The Bible says that God's voice makes deer give birth (Ps 29:9). It is normal that His voice acts on your soul and body. This being said, don't think that if you don'have these emotions or reactions , you must reject what you receive. The criteria are not your reactions, but what the Bible says about them.

Rely on his Word, God is waiting for you.

Once you have received by faith what you believe comes from God, dive into the Bible to see if it is biblical. Only after this examination ,you will be able to remember what is good and drink the water of the river that flows through you by the Holy Spirit. Biblical confirmations will support your faith and prevent you from mistaking your thoughts or those of the devil from those of God.

God has given us his Word as a guide. The Bible is THE Word of God, inspired by the Holy Spirit. You must rely on it to filter and inspire your spiritual experiences.

Filtering your spiritual experiences means that you must refuse to venture into spiritual experiences that would be opposed to the Bible. Many non-Christian people have spiritual experiences related to spiritualism, witchcraft, astral travel, etc.

> *No, I imply that what pagans sacrifice they offer to demons and not to God. I do not want you to be participants with demons. You cannot drink the cup of the Lord and the cup of demons. You cannot partake of the table of the Lord and the table of demons.*
> *(1 Corinthians 10:20-21)*

The apostle Paul speaks here of meat sacrificed to idols in Gentile worship. These sacrifices could be accompanied by trances, visions or other prophecies. Paul is clear, we can have spiritual experiences that are demonically inspired, and it is to protect ourselves from this that we must examine things through the filter of the Bible. This examination can be done a priori: if we know that a certain practice is not biblical, there is no need to taste it. For example, the Bible condemns praying to the dead, so there is no need to try it.

This examination must also be done after the fact. If I am praying and I have a vision for example, I must check that the vision is biblical once it is finished.

But even if we or an angel from heaven should preach to you a gospel contrary to the one we preached to you, let him be accursed. As we have said before, so now I say again: If anyone is preaching to you a gospel contrary to the one you received, let him be accursed.
(Galatians 1.8-9)

Many sects and heresies have come from a person who ,at one time, had a vision or met a shining angel. Despite the fact that the content of the message was opposed to the Bible, people began to believe these things without further examination because of the spiritual nature of the vision. But we know that God will never contradict His Word.

And no wonder, for even Satan disguises himself as an angel of light.
(2 Corinthians 11:14)

What will protect you from coming into contact with demons, what will protect you from the enemy's wiles and deception, is to examine all spiritual experience in the light of the Bible.

I like to use the image of the trampoline. A trampoline allows you to jump high and do acrobatic tricks. The deeper you go into a trampoline, the higher you bounce. In the same way, the Bible inspires our spiritual experiences. The more we dive into the Word of God, the more we discover the mysteries of God, the more we experience with the Holy Spirit. These experiences may seem «acrobatic» to rational thinking, such as healing the sick, speaking in tongues or receiving words of knowledge. But as long as you fall back on the trampoline (the Bible), you are safe. What is dangerous is to jump on a trampoline, do a back somersault and fall back on your back, on the ground next to the trampoline. Don't let the sensational (feeling) aspect prevent you from examining whether what you are experiencing is biblical.

The Bible shows you how God speaks, how you should react and what you should not do. Indeed, we see in the lives of biblical characters their mistakes and steps of faith. Would you like to pray with me?

Lord, I bring to you my fears and ignorance. I come to you as a child. In the same way that I managed to speak English, I believe that you are leading me to learn to speak the language of the Holy Spirit. I choose to persevere. Thank you because you are with me and I can make mistakes. In the name of Jesus, Amen.

I pray for you:

Lord, I bless my brother/sister who comes to you with thirst. I bless what you have already done in him/her and I pray for more. May the streams of water become torrents in him/her. I release your peace, your Shalom so that he/she can be quiet inside. I pray that he/she will think clearly and that a deposit of faith and perseverance will be communicated to him/her. May the enemy be unmasked and may he/she fully experience the joy of being guided by you.In the name of Jesus, Amen.

Practice exercise

Now it's time to put into practice what you've just read! Relax physically and mentally and take your journal to write down what you will receive. Play some instrumental music, for example by scanning this code with your phone or by typing the following address: entdi.eu/piano

Focus your attention on Jesus and then say:

«Lord, here I am, speak, your child is listening. »

Focus on the Holy Spirit within you and write one of the following questions:

«Lord, how do you see me? »

«What do you want to tell me today? »

Do not try to analyze while you are receiving. Remain in simple faith, like a child, while you receive. Once you have finished (give yourself time, at least ten minutes), examine what you have received.

- ·What has this produced in you?
- ·Does the Bible agree what you have received?

CHAPTER 4.

RECEIVING VISIONS

I never cease to give thanks for you; I mention you in my prayers, that the God of our Lord Jesus Christ, the Father of glory, may give you a spirit of wisdom and revelation in his knowledge; that he may enlighten the eyes of your heart.

(Ephesians 1:16-18).

These are the things I received from the Lord as I listened to him in preparing this chapter:

I want to open your eyes to show you what I do. My Spirit reveals and shows you spiritual realities. Accept what I show you. Expect to see what I will show you. Let yourself be led by me.

God wants to open your spiritual eyes

Paul prayed that the eyes of the believers' hearts would be illuminated. This prayer was intended for all Christians, because the letter to the Ephesians was a circular epistle, to be copied and read in other churches. Therefore, Paul's prayer is still valid for us today.

When the apostle prays for the eyes of the heart to be illuminated, he talks about the spiritual eyes. First of all, this informs us that we have spiritual eyes to see spiritual things.

Our eyes can be closed

having the eyes of your hearts enlightened, that you may know what is the hope to which he has called you, what are the riches of his glorious inheritance in the saints.

(Ephesians 1:18)

If Paul prays for our eyes to be opened, it is because they can be closed. We can see physically and be blind spiritually. This is what Jesus will say about the people who listened to his teachings:

For this people's heart has grown dull, and with their ears they can barely hear, and their eyes they have closed, lest they should see with their eyes and hear with their ears and understand with their heart and turn, and I would heal them. 'But blessed are your eyes, for they see, and your ears, for they hear.

(Matthew 13:15-16)

When Jesus taught, some understood and some did not. When Jesus says that they closed their eyes, he is not talking about physical eyes, but spiritual eyes. When we refer to the different versions, we see that it is about insensitivity, thickening of the heart or numbness. Literally, we can speak of a callus of the heart. Rationalism and averseness are, in my opinion, at the origin of this blindness. Rationalism refuses everything, rationalism cannot understand and limits itself to the physical world to explain everything. Unbelief refuses to believe what God says and to trust Him. The spiritual eyes of the heart serve to perceive spiritual realities. It is through the eyes of the heart that one receives revelations. If our eyes are closed, then we will not be able to grasp what God wants to communicate to us in vision, we will be limited in our understanding of our heritage. If we are not aware of our heritage and what is available in God for us, we will not be able to access it through faith. It is therefore a necessity that our spiritual eyes are opened.

Many other things can close our eyes: ignorance, fear or our will.

Now concerning spiritual gifts, brothers, I do not want you to be uninformed.

(1 Corinthians 12:1)

Paul says he doesn't want us to be ignorant about spiritual gifts. When we don't know that God is speaking, like Samuel, we don't think to answer Him if he calls us. When we don't know that we can receive visions, we don't think that an image that we have in our thoughts can come from God and so we don't pay attention to it.

For God speaks in one way, and in two, though man does not perceive it.

(Job 33:14)

Visions are often sweet and light, and can easily be ignored, like God's thoughts. By ignoring them, we deprive ourselves of what they were meant to reveal to us. To be attentive to what God shows us, we must have faith that He will give us visions. Faith is based on the invisible, but it is an assurance of invisible things, not a hope. This assurance comes from the knowledge of the truth revealed in God's Word.

> *And in the last days it shall be, God declares, that I will pour out my Spirit on all flesh, and your sons and your daughters shall prophesy, and your young men shall see visions, and your old men shall dream dreams*
>
> *(Acts of the Apostles 2.17)*

Peter is clear when he quotes the prophet Joel on the day of Pentecost. It is normal for a Spirit-filled Christian to have visions and dreams. Visions are images received when we are awake, while dreams are images received when we are asleep. So we can rely with faith on this promise and expect to receive visions from God.

When we see something that is not rational, we may believe that we are hallucinating, we may even be afraid to share what we have seen for fear of other people's reactions. I often talk to people who have asked God to stop seeing the spiritual world, they have closed their eyes. They didn't know what to do with what they saw. For someone who has never had a vision, it may seem exaggerated to talk about fear, but when you read the Bible, you realize that the visions God gives can be very emotionally intense.

When God shows what He is doing in a vision, the impact is real and lasting in a person's life. It's like a download. The vision captures spiritual realities. Here is Helene's testimony to illustrate this point:

I was raised in a Jehovah's Witness family. When I grew up and left them, I was unable to trust the Bible and those who taught it. Furthermore, I could not taste God's peace, nor could I grasp His promises, let alone call God my Father. I knew he loved me, but only in my head, not in my heart. One Sunday I prayed once again to taste his love and peace (I had been praying about this for several years). The worship team brought a first song called «Christ is King» and during this song I saw a white cloud in the church going up to heaven. There were angels ascending and descending from this cloud. Afterwards, I saw angels near each of the people in the church. As the time of praise continued, I continued to see the cloud and the angels ascending and descending from heaven. A second time we sang «Christ is King» and I began to cry and pray to God to taste His love and peace. Then an angel took me and brought me to heaven. I couldn't see anything because I had to remain prostrate in the cloud. A voice spoke to me and told me that I was his daughter, his child, that he loved me. Then the angel brought me back to the church and I saw my heart in a cage. Jesus came close to the cage and the cage broke. God had set my heart free. Then I felt God's love like I had never felt before. After this vision, I changed a lot. I am now able to empathize with people and make the words of the Bible my own. I no longer doubt my salvation. I can taste God's love and peace. I know now that I am Her child, and this is an assurance in my heart. Two weeks later, I was in church again. We were singing, and something (surely the Holy Spirit) made me go forward and sing with those who had come out of the ranks. For me it was something huge, because I am a very shy person. I really didn't want to go, but the voice was insistent, I had to go and sing ahead. So I ended up listening to it. When I got to the front, I saw an angel next to me who reassured me. After a few minutes, during a song, I began to speak in tongues for the first time. I felt like a power within me and I spoke in tongues the rest of the song.

Sometimes those who had visions shared what they had seen and were not taken seriously. Similarly, it is possible that a child has had visions and his parents have tried to rationalize them, blaming it on imagination instead of recognizing their child's real spiritual sensitivity. Unfortunately, often the consequence is that the child then decides to voluntarily close his or her spiritual eyes because he or she was not believed.

No matter what has closed your spiritual eyes so far, God can open them in response to prayer. It is therefore normal, as Paul did, to pray for our eyes to open to the spiritual world. Remember that the Lord created you with spiritual eyes and it is His will that you have visions.

So I invite you to pray now so that your spiritual eyes may open:

Lord Jesus, please open my spiritual eyes. I ask your forgiveness for all the times you have revealed things to me without my knowledge. I forgive those who did not believe me. I believe that you want to give me visions and I expect this. I renounce all fear and trust you in the name of Jesus, Amen.

Spiritual vision can develop

having the eyes of your hearts enlightened, that you may know what is the hope to which he has called you, what are the riches of his glorious inheritance in the saints.

(Ephesians 1:18)

Receiving visions, like hearing God's voice in our thoughts, is a learning process. God is the source of what He shows us, but our learning will allow us to better recognize what He reveals to us and, above all, to know what to do with it. We can pray to see more precisely and more often. This spiritual acuity can also be developed by associating fasting with prayer. Personally, I had my first vision with my eyes open while I had been fasting for several days. I was in my basement praying and listening to praise. As I looked at the wall in front of me, I suddenly saw a huge forest fire. I was on the edge of the fire and tried to put it out with a fire hose, but I could not cope with the magnitude of the task. Around me, I saw people who were facing the fire and had nothing to put it out. Behind me I saw piles of coiled fire hoses. I unrolled them and gave them to the people and then connected the hoses to a huge pump that drew water from a river. When the water got into the hoses, the pressure was so high that people had trouble holding the hoses, the water was spilling everywhere, but the more thoses people had ,the more the fire receded. I understood that fire represented the works of the devil and that the distribution of fire hoses was to equip people with spiritual gifts, lay hands on them and communicate the power of God. I then noted in my journal, «Do not lay hands on people if they are not ready. Then I asked God what he wanted to tell me about this. He said, «We must not be afraid that people will make mistakes. As long as there is water to put out the fire, it is better than nothing. Everyone will have to learn too. «I looked again and saw that finally people were able to control the fire hoses and direct the water to the fire. I realized that God was showing me this vision to encourage me to do what I would naturally have had to do, which is to pray for as many people as possible to be clothed in the power of the Holy Spirit. I remembered several things that day. First of all, we must look to see what God is showing us. What He shows us must be interpreted with His help, for we can understand the opposite of what He wants to tell us. So it is possible in the learning process that I may be wrong, because I did not interpret what God was showing me. Interpretation is as important as revelation. On the other hand, I found that when we look carefully, we can see the rest of the vision.

God wants to show you what He does

So, Jesus said to them, "Truly, truly, I say to you, the Son can do nothing of his own accord, but only what he sees the Father doing. For whatever the Father does, that the Son does likewise.

(John 5.19)

Jesus did what he saw his Father doing. So the reason Jesus had such diverse methods is because he had different visions of what God was doing. Visions are used to see what God is doing and to grasp spiritual realities. This verse instructs us in many ways. Let us remember that God wants to collaborate with us and show us what we should do with Him. What he reveals to us should move us into action. So we need to learn to act on what he shows us. If you want to live more with God, look at what he shows you and do it. One day I was praying for a man. I wanted him to respond to a call to the altar. Then I received a vision, like a flash, in my mind. I saw myself taking him in my arms and hugging him. To put this in context, I didn't know much about him and was not used to hugging men, the Canadian embrace being already out of my comfort zone. Inside, I began to pray, «Lord, is that you? I can't hug him, I'm not comfortable! «This image remained insistent. I thought that it was a way to make concrete the love of God the Father for this man, to be God's arms for a moment. After a few seconds of hesitation, I decided to obey and take the risk of doing what God had shown me. I asked the man's permission to take him in my arms. He agreed and I hugged him. God showed me after a few seconds that I had to put my head on his shoulder. I obeyed with some reluctance and prayed that he would experience the Father's love, his embrace. The Bible tells us that the Holy Spirit communicates the Father's love. So I invited the Holy Spirit to come and fill this man with love and waited. After a few moments, he began to cry. The Lord was working in his heart. He was sobbing in my arms with tears. After a while, I heard in my mind that God was saying to me, «It's okay, you can stop. This man was met by God on that day. God wanted to bless him, he had shown me what he wanted to do and I obeyed. Since that day, the Lord has asked me many times to hold men in my arms. When He shows me this image, the man in question is often reluctant to do so. But God's love makes hearts crack. What a joy to see men experiencing the love of their heavenly Father!

I would like to give you the list of images and associated actions, but it does not exist. God does not want you to learn a method, He wants to collaborate with you by developing a relationship of intimacy. He will show you things personally and you will learn to obey him by faith.

Expect to see what God will show you.

I will take my stand at my watch post and station myself on the tower, and look out to see what he will say to me, and what I will answer concerning my complaint. And the LORD answered me: "Write the vision; make it plain on tablets, so he may run who reads it.

(Habakkuk 2:1-2)

Habakkuk was a prophet who had visions. He explains in this verse what he does to receive visions: he first stands at his guard post. Likewise, it is good for us to have a guard-house, a place of regular appointment with God. A guard often spends whole nights watching, watching to see nothing, but he is attentive. When you stand before the Lord, you must be attentive to what He will show you, for He wants to talk to you. Habakkuk has questions for God and he expects God to answer him with visions, so he watches carefully, waiting to receive something. It's obvious, but when you're watching, nothing happens until something happens! Faith allows us to wait for the answer. You will not have a vision every time you watch for God, but waiting for Him will certainly increase the number of visions you will receive. To increase your faith, therefore, you must decide to wait longer before Him.

Once Habakkuk has received the vision, God asks him to write it down. The goal is to retain it, to be able to meditate on it while having precise details. In the same way, you too can describe or draw your vision. I encourage you to keep a diary in which you will collect the visions you have had. This will give you encouragement. Most French versions translate «so that it is read fluently»; this is one of the purposes of keeping a written record of a vision. But the Darby version translates verse 2 this way:

And the LORD answered me: "Write the vision; make it plain on tablets, so he may run who reads it.

(Habakkuk 2.2)

Habakkuk announces the arrival of the Chaldeans who will ravage the country. The visions that God gives him explain the reasons for this: violence in the kingdom of Judah has reached its height. Since the vision is the announcement of the destruction of the country, Habakkuk prays and intercedes for God's compassion:

O LORD, I have heard the report of you, and your work, O LORD, do I fear. In the midst of the years revive it; in the midst of the years make it known; in wrath remember mercy.

(Habakkuk 3.2)

But since the vision must be written and shared, he who by faith takes this announcement seriously should run away! The point I want to draw your attention to here is that when visions are taken seriously, written down, they are meant to produce action in those who read or hear them.

There is a wide variety of visions

The content of the vision is of course limitless, but I want to mention different forms of visions in order to arouse your faith and reassure you if you experience something similar. Each of these visions can occur while waiting before God, in personal prayer, while you pray for someone or at any time in your daily life, as God sees fit.

Flash vision

The most subtle form of God's visions is a quick image in our mind, like a flash, which we catch in flight like a bird that passes quickly before our eyes. We may doubt that we saw something, we may have had trouble seeing the details. Faith intervenes in these kinds of visions. You have to expect to receive them and therefore take the risk of looking at what you have seen rapidly. You must then focus on the vision and ask God for the meaning or action associated with it.

As I was praying one morning, I saw a quick picture of new lamps on the ceiling of our church. A few days later, the owner of the premises came to replace the faulty lamps with a model that matched the one in the vision. At that time, I had not yet had a vision. I told God about it and He said, «I open your eyes to see what I am doing. «That was the beginning of my learning to see what God is doing. Having the physical confirmation of these lamps in front of my eyes increased my faith to expect to see more of what God wants to show me. Remember that what pleases God is your faith. It is necessary to exercise faith in order to believe a flash vision. So God likes to use these kinds of visions. Don't neglect them!

The persistent vision

This kind of vision is insistent, we can't ignore it. Like a butterfly circling in front of us. This insistence invites us to pay attention. Sometimes we have difficulty believing or doing what God shows us, so He insists. Other times, we don't know what to do with it. His insistence then leads us to ask ourselves what he expects of us.

An animated vision

Some visions are fixed, like a painting, others are animated, like a movie. One can be a spectator of the vision or an actor in the vision. The level of detail can be very varied.

A vision with open eyes

The previous types of visions are visible in our mind, with our eyes closed. But it is also possible to receive a vision that is superimposed on reality while our eyes are open. Recently, a friend wrote to me about this. He was talking with someone when the face of the person he was talking to was replaced before his eyes by a vision of me.

A vision of the spiritual world

Some visions are symbolic images, metaphors to communicate a truth, a message, a directive. Others are outright a vision of the spiritual world. In this kind of vision, we can see Jesus, angels, demons. Someone may have a vision of this type on an ad hoc basis or very frequently to the point of seeing into the spiritual world on demand. We then speak of a gift of clairvoyance. This word is often associated with the occult, but did you know that Samuel was a seer ? In fact, nine biblical characters are called seers in the Bible , not to mention those who have visions without being so designated. This is the case of the prophet Elisha who saw the spiritual world.

Then Elisha prayed and said, "O LORD, please open his eyes that he may see." So the LORD opened the eyes of the young man, and he saw, and behold, the mountain was full of horses and chariots of fire all around Elisha.

(2 Kings 6:17)

In the Second Book of Kings, we see that Elisha heard in spirit the plans of the king of Syria and repeated them to the king of Israel. This happened so often that the news reached the ears of the king of Syria. Everyone knew that God was speaking to Elisha, even his enemies. The king decided to send a whole army to capture the prophet. When his servant came out of the house, he found an army surrounding him and became afraid. Elisha reassured him because he could see the chariots of God's fire around him sent to protect them.

He said, "Do not be afraid, for those who are with us are more than those who are with them."

(2 Kings 6.16)

Not only did Elisha see the chariots of God, but also the demons that accompanied their enemies, for he declared, «Those who are with them. "It is easy to conclude that the prophet had a spiritual vision of the angelic world. An invisible world, but very real. He prayed for his servant who then had the same vision of the chariots of fire. This prayer is the same as that of Paul: «Lord, open his eyes, that he may see. «As you read these lines, I pray that God will open your spiritual eyes so that you can thwart the enemy's plans and see what God is doing.

Travelling in spirit

We can live a spiritual journey in which God takes us somewhere in spirit to show us something. It happened to Ezekiel and God can do it for you too.

In the sixth year, in the sixth month, on the fifth day of the month, as I sat in my house, with the elders of Judah sitting before me, the hand of the Lord GOD fell upon me there. Then I looked, and behold, a form that had the appearance of a man. Below what appeared to be his waist was fire, and above his waist was something like the appearance of brightness, like gleaming metal. He put out the form of a hand and took me by a lock of my head, and the Spirit lifted me up between earth and heaven and brought me in visions of God to Jerusalem, to the entrance of the gateway of the inner court that faces north, where was the seat of the image of jealousy, which provokes to jealousy.

(Ezekiel 8.1-3)

Ezekiel is not praying, it is God who sovereignly comes to meet him. I mention this passage to broaden your expectation and quench your thirst. In this experience, Ezekiel has a vision with his eyes open, and of a spiritual being who interacts with him and transports him, shows him visions and speaks to him. It is possible to experience these things even if you are a beginner, it is God who decides. Don't think that these experiences are reserved for an elite. Isaiah began his ministry with the vision he tells in the sixth chapter of his book. He has a vision of God on his throne, and he sees and hears the seraphim who worship him. He feels the ground vibrating beneath his feet at the sound of their voices. An angel comes to touch him and God interacts with him. There are in fact no limits to what God can show you. You just have to watch out for him. Focus on what you see, and let the Lord guide you in the vision.

The Holy Spirit reveals and shows you spiritual realities, welcome what He shows you.

If you believe that God wants to give you visions, then by faith you will have to accept what he will show you. Welcoming means considering the value of the vision. It's not just an image, you have to meditate on it, there is a reason why God has given you this vision. There is a major difference between the visions of our imagination and the visions of God. If I ask you to imagine a pink elephant, you can have a mental image of it, but that image will not change you. On the other hand, God's visions are spontaneous and can communicate an entire concept to us, comfort us lastingly, mark us deeply, encourage us. A picture is worth a thousand words. God created us with the ability to learn through metaphors, we are able to make connections between related concepts. That is why God also uses representations as a powerful means to reveal his mysteries to us. We tend to remember an image more easily than a sentence. When we welcome what the Lord shows us, it is like a download from heaven within us. When we share a vision of God, those who hear it can feel the effect in their minds. For example, I often tell about the vision I received of the forest fire and the fire hoses before praying for spiritual gifts for people. This inspires faith and announces what God is going to do.

Welcoming the vision also means focusing.

And I saw in the vision; and when I saw, I was in Susa the citadel, which is in the province of Elam. And I saw in the vision, and I was at the Ulai canal..

(Daniel 8:2)

When we listen to someone, we use the expression «active listening» which means paying close attention to understand what is being said, also taking into account the non-verbal language of the speaker. When God gives you a vision, you need to look actively, attentively, focused on what He is showing you. Daniel was looking into the vision. He was not passive. Imagine that God's vision is a picture in a room in your mind. You can see the picture from a distance or you can get close to it and appreciate every detail. It is this sustained attention that will allow you to receive all that God wants to communicate to you. Faith is the support for this attention, because your mind may think it is just your imagination.

The Holy Spirit reveals the mysteries of God

But, as it is written, "What no eye has seen, nor ear heard nor the heart of man imagined, what God has prepared for those who love him"—these things God has revealed to us through the Spirit. For the Spirit searches everything, even the depths of God. For who knows a person's thoughts except the spirit of that person, which is in him? So also no one comprehends the thoughts of God except the Spirit of God. Now we have received not the spirit of the world, but the Spirit who is from God, that we might understand the things freely given us by God.

(1 Corinthians 2:9-12)

Revealing means making known to someone or making public what was kept secret. God reveals to us by His Spirit what is a secret to man without God. It is like lifting a veil so that we can see what exists but which we did not see. The Lord, by His grace, has given us much more than we are aware of. If you accept His visions, He will reveal what is yours for you to enjoy.

It is God who reveals, we just make people look and receive the revelation. When we receive it, it becomes a truth for us, it is imprinted, it becomes integrated in us, we never go back to ignorance and we can then act on it. This is what makes us progress in successive stages, from revelation to revelation.

Let yourself be led by the Holy Spirit

Remember that it is God who reveals, He is the source of the visions, so stay in His rest and ask Him to lead you, to explain, to tell you what to do with what you have seen.

You will have images that are clear and easy to understand. Let's take the example of the lady who asked God what her value was and saw a chest full of gold coins. This means that she is precious like a treasure for God. If you have a vision of a person you know who needs help, pray for her and ask about her.

Some images are symbolic and simple to interpret. This can be for example a biblical symbol such as the cross, oil, a dove, a tree bearing fruit, a snake. You will then first have to write down the vision and then find the interpretation. This will allow you to reread the basic vision if you are wrong in your interpretation, so that instead of believing that it did not come from God, you will learn to interpret it better. The ideal is to ask God for the meaning.

You will also have mysterious visions that will require God's explanation.

> *And the word of the LORD came to me, saying, "Jeremiah, what do you see?" And I said, "I see an almond branch." Then the LORD said to me, "You have seen well, for I am watching over my word to perform it."*
>
> *(Jeremiah 1.11-12)*

The word «almond tree» and the word «watch» have the same root in Hebrew, so these two words are in harmony. God speaks to Jeremiah with puns. Remember that he is the author of the visions so he is the one who holds the meaning. He is very creative!

The Lord loves to lead us to the discovery of His mysteries like a father who prepared a treasure hunt for his children. His goal is that they will be in the joy of discovering the treasure after a little effort and research.

It is possible that you may have the meaning within you as well as the vision. The Lord himself may give you this interpretation You must be sensitive to it. Having said that, it is always good to ask God, because we can have our own interpretations that are distorted.

I invite you to pray with me:

Father, I consecrate my eyes to you now, I ask you to purify them and I decide by faith to expect to receive visions from you. I choose to watch before you to see what you will show me. Guide me and reveal yourself to me in the name of Jesus, Amen.

I pray for you now:

Father, I beg you to open the eyes of your son/daughter so that he/she may have visions. Holy Spirit, come upon him/her now, that he/she may see what you are doing, reveal to him/her the mysteries that you reveal to your children. In the name of Jesus, Amen.

Take time to receive a vision from God. Remain a few minutes in silence, the time for instrumental music. Click on the following address:

entdi.eu / piano

Say:

«Lord, here I am, what do you want to show me? »

Close your eyes and watch for what Jesus will show you.

- What has this produced in you?
- Does the Bible support what you have received?

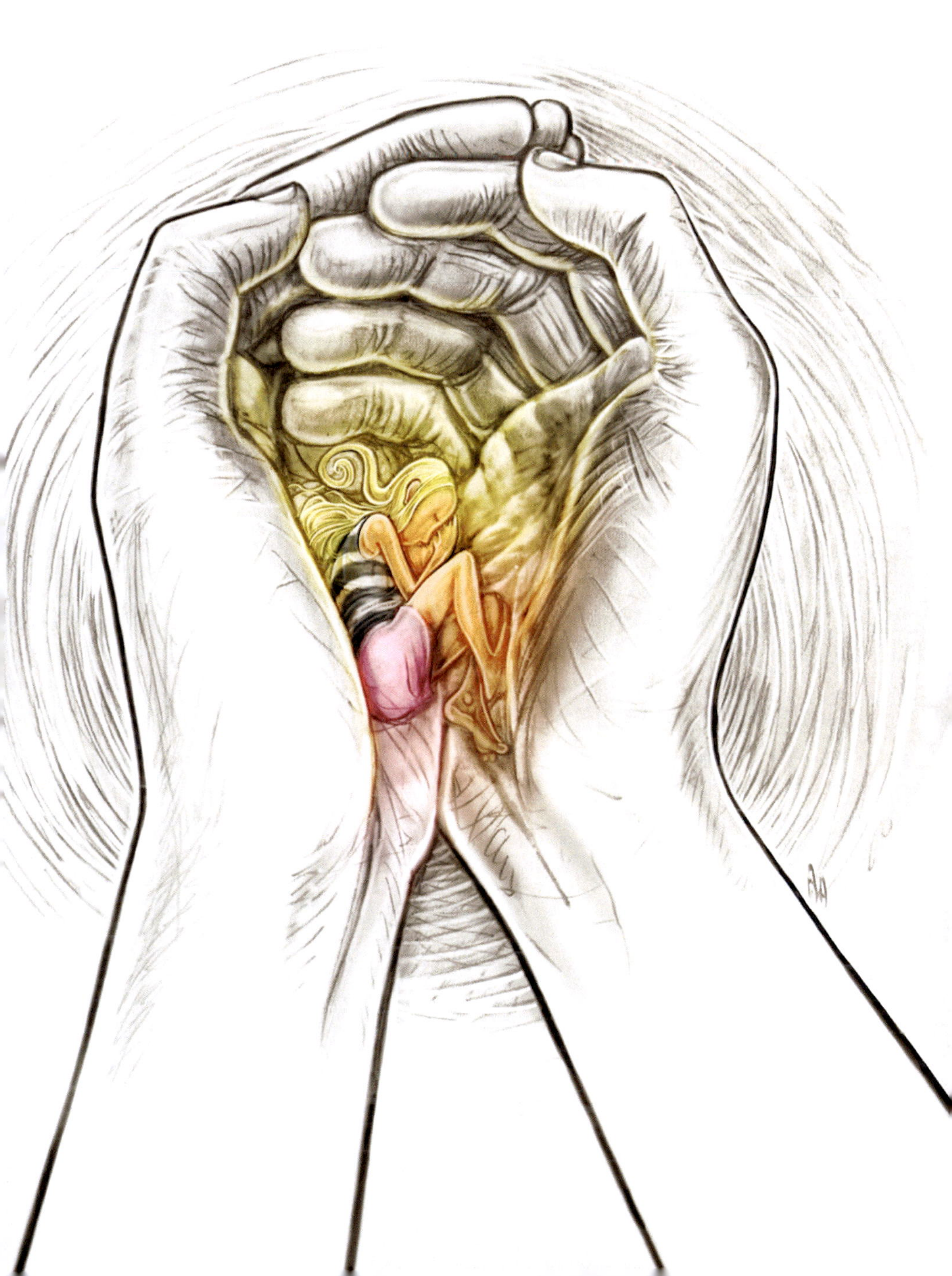

CHAPTER 5.

TASTE THE MANIFESTATION OF HIS PRESENCE

Whoever has my commandments and keeps them, he it is who loves me. And he who loves me will be loved by my Father, and I will love him and manifest myself to him.

(John 14:21)

These are the things I received from the Lord as I listened to him in preparing this chapter:

It is I who created you. I can touch every part of your being. When two people are in communion, they exchange, laughter or experience emotions together and also communicate phy-sically. I love to hold my children in my arms. Receive my affection.

It is God who created you ; He can touch every part of your being.

When I dedicated myself to searching for God with all my heart at the age of 19, I spent time alone in my room listening to praise; I prayed, read the Bible, and also had times of silence before God. I remember a song by Sandra Clark that said, «In your presence, in silence, I wait. Sitting at your feet, my thoughts to you rise. What do you have to say to me? I want to listen to the sound of your voice. «I remember experiencing physical manifestations of God's presence in these moments. I felt my face tingle as if I was in the sun, I felt a weight in my hands as if God was putting something on it. I felt as if I was enveloped by the Lord. I had no explanation for this and no one around me mentioned this kind of experience. So I kept them to myself. As the years went by and a few Bible school classes later, I lost this sense of the tangible manifestation of God's presence to a more intellectual approach. When I began to listen to God's voice, these experiences began again and grew.

How about taking a break, now, for a time of silence before God?

God created you and He knows how to get your attention, even if you don't hear or see Him. It is important to recognize when God is showing Himself to you, when He is touching you. If He is calling you and you are not paying attention, you may miss a moment with Him.

That very day two of them were going to a village named Emmaus, about seven miles from Jerusalem, and they were talking with each other about all these things that had happened. While they were talking and discussing together, Jesus himself drew near and went with them. But their eyes were kept from recognizing him. And he said to them, "What is this conversation that you are holding with each other as you walk?" And they stood still, looking sad. Then one of them, named Cleopas, answered him, "Are you the only visitor to Jerusalem who does not know the things that have happened there in these days?" And he said to them, "What things?" And they said to him, "Concerning Jesus of Nazareth, a man who was a prophet mighty in deed and word before God and all the people, and how our chief priests and rulers delivered him up to be condemned to death, and crucified him. But we had hoped that he was the one to redeem Israel. Yes, and besides all this, it is now the third day since these things happened. Moreover, some women of our company amazed us. They were at the tomb early in the morning, and when they did not find his body, they came back saying that they had even seen a vision of angels, who said that he was alive. Some of those who were with us went to the tomb and found it just as the women had said, but him they did not see." And he said to them, "O foolish ones, and slow of heart to believe all that the prophets have spoken! Was it not necessary that the Christ should suffer these things and enter into his glory?" And beginning with Moses and all the Prophets, he interpreted to them in all the Scriptures the things concerning himself.

So they drew near to the village to which they were going. He acted as if he were going farther, but they urged him strongly, saying, "Stay with us, for it is toward evening and the day is now far spent." So he went in to stay with them. When he was at table with them, he took the bread and blessed and broke it and gave it to them. And their eyes were opened, and they recognized him. And he vanished from their sight. They said to each other, "Did not our hearts burn within us while he talked to us on the road, while he opened to us the Scriptures?" And they rose that same hour and returned to Jerusalem. And they found the eleven and those who were with them gathered together, saying, "The Lord has risen indeed, and has appeared to Simon!" Then they told what had happened on the road, and how he was known to them in the breaking of the bread.

(Luke 24:13-35)

Jesus revealed Himself clearly to Peter, Mary, Thomas, but this time He manifested Himself differently to Cleopas and his friend. These two men could not believe that Jesus was alive despite the testimony of the empty tomb. They could neither believe the women who said they saw him nor the message of the angels. They told Jesus, «But they did not see him,» even though he was standing before them. Their eyes were closed and they did not recognize the Lord. Jesus had to overcome many obstacles so that his disciples could finally recognize him.

Your emotions can close your spiritual eyes

But we had hoped that he was the one to redeem Israel. Yes, and besides all this, it is now the third day since these things happened.
(Luke 24:21)

Emotional barriers closed their spiritual eyes. They were sad, disappointed and discouraged after Jesus' death. Likewise, sometimes our emotions are so strong that they prevent us from connecting with God. When a child cries, it is often not the time for constructive dialogue. A wise parent will take his or her child in his or her arms, consoling him or her, caressing him/her, hugging him/her, running his /her hand through his/her hair. These gestures of tenderness will allow the child to receive the comfort that they cannot get from words. In the same way, God knows how to overcome the emotional obstacles in our lives by manifesting Himself to us in a comforting way, He can touch us in spite of our pain.

Ignorance and misconceptions can close your spiritual eyes.

And he said to them, "O foolish ones, and slow of heart to believe all that the prophets have spoken!

(Luke 24:25)

The disciples did not understand why Jesus had died. So he began by explaining the Scriptures to them in order to change their thoughts. It is, in fact, more difficult to see or recognize something that one cannot conceive of. Your faith can only be based on a good understanding of God's Word. For example, now that you know you can have visions, you will more easily grasp what God is showing you instead of believing it is your imagination. In the same way, you can recognize Jesus at your side if you believe what the Bible says, that is, that He wants to show Himself to you. I think Cleopas must have been used to feeling his heart burning when Jesus was teaching. Nothing compares to that.

They said to each other, "Did not our hearts burn within us while he talked to us on the road, while he opened to us the Scriptures?"

(Luke 24:32)

The disciples, feeling their hearts burning within them, had an inner testimony that confirmed that Jesus's words were very true. This presence was a confirmation.

Disbelief can close your spiritual eyes

Finally, these two disciples found it hard to believe. When you think about it, the resurrection is beyond understanding.. They had seen Jesus crucified. Their intelligence could not conceive that he was alive. Yet, when Jesus broke the bread, their eyes were opened and the Lord disappeared before their eyes. What allowed them to believe that it was Jesus and not a hallucination was the physical and emotional sensation they both felt. Their hearts were burning! That fire rekindled their faith. They had not believed the women who had met the angels, but because of what they had just experienced, they immediately returned to Jerusalem to announce that they had seen the living Jesus. They felt that they could rely on what they had felt to confirm what they thought they had seen.

> *Whoever has my commandments and keeps them, he it is who loves me. And he who loves me will be loved by my Father, and I will love him and manifest myself to him.*
>
> *(John 14:21)*

The verb manifest means: «to make perceptible, to make known a feeling». We must therefore expect, since it is a promise of Jesus, to perceive also through our senses and emotions the manifestation of God's presence.

God wants to communicate with you, whether you are ready or not, whether you understand Him or not, whether you are willing or not. He uses every means to get your attention and to share His love with you. If you welcome the manifestation of his presence, you will enter into greater communion with him.

When two people are in communion, they exchange, laugh or experience emotions together and also communicate physically.

Jesus promised that he would show himself to the one who loves him. Being sensitive to the possibility of Jesus' presence in our lives allows us to recognize and welcome him, even if we do not yet hear or see him. Jesus promised to show Himself to the one who loves Him, but He does not say precisely how. You can expect Him to touch your emotions and your body. From one person to another, the manifestation of God will be different. So it is up to you to discover and recognize how the Lord represents Himself to you. You can have many experiences with the Holy Spirit in your intimacy with Him.

Regarding the manifestations of the Holy Spirit in public, be aware that there is a difference between experiencing God's presence personally and blessing those around you with the anointing of the Holy Spirit. It is necessary to make a difference between the manifestation of God that are reactions of our body or soul to God's presence and the manifestation of the Holy Spirit that are intended to edify those around us. Although the same word is used in the Bible, they are two different realities.

When Jesus says that he will manifest himself to the one who believes in him, the Greek word is «emphanizo». It means «to manifest, to appear, to make known». It is used, for example, for the appearance of the resurrected Jesus after His crucifixion.

> *and coming out of the tombs after his resurrection they went into the holy city and appeared (emphanizo) to many.*
>
> *(Matthew 27:53)*

«Emphanizo» is the verb taken from the noun «emphanes» which is used for the appearance of Jesus to his disciples.

> *but God raised him on the third day and made him to appear (emphanes), not to all the people but to us who had been chosen by God as witnesses, who ate and drank with him after he rose from the dead.*
>
> *(Acts of the Apostles 10:40-41).*

It can be said that the purpose of an «emphanizo» manifestation is to convince the one who lives this manifestation of its origin. This verb is also translated as «to appear before a court», an exercise whose purpose is to convince the judge and the jury.

> *And after five days the high priest Ananias came down with some elders and a spokesman, one Tertullus. They laid before the governor their case (emphanizo) against Paul.*
>
> *(Acts of the Apostles 24.1)*

On the other hand, when the Apostle Paul speaks of the manifestation of the Spirit concerning spiritual gifts, he uses the word «phanerosis», which is used only twice in the New Testament.

> *To each is given the manifestation (phanerosis) of the Spirit for the common good.*

(1 Corinthians 12:7)

«Phanerosis» also has the meaning of publishing, which is how it is translated in the other verse where it appears:

But we have renounced disgraceful, underhanded ways. We refuse to practice cunning or to tamper with God's word, but by the open statement of the truth (phanerosis) we would commend ourselves to everyone's conscience in the sight of God.

(2 Corinthians 4:2)

Darby translated as «by the manifestation of the truth»; the Segond version translated as «by publishing the truth»; the Modern French Bible Translation as «we make the truth clearly known». The notion here is to communicate something to others clearly. This is the purpose of spiritual gifts.

If the manifestation of God («emphanizo») is a reaction of my body to the action of God in me, I must welcome it and let it do what it wants in me (comfort, inner healing, power equipping, deliverance...) without seeking to attract the attention of others, since the manifestation is for me.

Here is the testimony of an Internet user who has viewed a teaching from my YouTube channel. He tells what he experienced during a time of prayer.

I was in my room following the teaching on the transfer of anointing by laying on of hands by Pastor David Théry. When he began to communicate the anointing to us, it was great. I was shaking with all my limbs: arms, neck, head. My hands were facing upwards as if I was receiving while I was shaking. I was shivering, I felt as if there was a weight in my hands. The more I shivered, the more that weight increased in each of my open hands. A sound came out of me as if I was groaning. It was a very pleasant atmosphere. Was it peace or joy or rest? I can't describe this atmosphere that lasted more than fifteen minutes. The more the pastor said, «more Lord,» the more I felt this state. Then I started to cry. Was it joy or peace? I don't know how to define the situation. It was the first time it had happened to me, but it was very pleasant. I can't describe exactly what it was. I had written to Pastor Théry to tell him that I didn't feel anything, that I didn't see anything as an image. I was disappointed, but not discouraged. I persevered and yesterdayI had divine manifestations. I am proud and joyful and above all grateful to God who loves me like all his children. I glorify him, may all the honor return to Him.

On the day of Pentecost, there were several manifestations of God's presence: the sound of a strong wind, visible flames of fire, drunkenness.

When the day of Pentecost arrived, they were all together in one place. And suddenly there came from heaven a sound like a mighty rushing wind, and it filled the entire house where they were sitting. And divided tongues as of fire appeared to them and rested on each one of them. And they were all filled with the Holy Spirit and began to speak in other tongues as the Spirit gave them utterance.

(Acts of the Apostles 2:1-4)

But others mocking said, "They are filled with new wine."
(Acts of the Apostles 2:13)

The apostle Peter explained to the Jews gathered around the disciples that the 120 were not drunk with wine, but filled with the Holy Spirit. However, his preaching was not based on these manifestations, but on the proclamation of the Gospel. The right biblical balance is to welcome the manifestation of the Holy Spirit, to give the biblical explanation of it, and to focus on the proclamation of the Gospel, which alone can save those around us. To reject the manifestations of the Holy Spirit is to reject the person of the Holy Spirit or to limit Him in what He wants to do in us. On the other hand, focusing only on the manifestations makes us lose sight of the purpose, the reason for this anointing of power, which is to be a witness of Jesus Christ. If you tremble under the anointing of the Holy Spirit and he gives you a message to share, the people around you will not be blessed by seeing you tremble, but by hearing the prophetic word. If you feel fire in your hands and simply tell those around you, it will at best spark curiosity and wonder. But if you lay your hands on them so that they may be healed, then you will reach God's goal. To conclude, when you feel the manifestation of the Holy Spirit in public, ask God what He wants from you, obey Him by faith and share what you have received, communicate to those around you the outpouring of God's anointing on your life.

> *You prepare a table before me in the presence of my enemies; you anoint my head with oil; my cup overflows.*
>
> *(Psalms 23:5)*

Now I want to give several examples of manifestations because often Christians experience them without daring to speak about them for fear of being rejected or because of ignorance. Let us begin with physical manifestations.

Crying before God

One of the most common physical manifestations of God's presence is crying. You are praising God or praying and start crying for no apparent reason. If you don't understand that God is touching you, then you may stop praying because you feel uncomfortable crying, or think you have a problem. But if you understand Jesus' promise to manifest Himself to you, you can welcome His presence in your life, focus on Him and enjoy a time of fellowship and intimacy with God. I have a friend who cries as soon as he starts to pray. When he feels the tears coming, he focuses on God's presence.

The warmth of God's presence

Another common manifestation is feeling heat on the body, on the hands or in the heart. This is what happened to the disciples on the road to Emmaus.

This warmth can manifest itself on you when you pray, it can be very localized or diffused. For example, personally, I very frequently feel heat on my forehead. At first it was like a spot between my eyes, after a while it developed on my forehead.

I told God about it and he gave me a picture. I saw a small flame, like the pilot flame or the pilot light of a gas boiler. The Lord explained to me that it was a manifestation of His presence, a way of telling me «I am here», of encouraging me or reassuring me depending on the circumstances. He then reminded me that I could count on Him and pray with confidence because He was with me. As the flame of the pilot light ensures that the boiler lights when the thermostat calls for it.

Many servants of God also feel warmth in their hands as an indication to pray for the sick.

It is also possible, as you pray for someone, that that person may feel the warmth of God's manifest presence in his or her body. This is a sign that the Holy Spirit is working in them. Just simply pray to bless what God is doing, pray that it will intensify, pray that what the Lord has begun will be fully accomplished.

Radiating the glory of God

Moses' face shone as he left the presence of God.

When Moses came down from Mount Sinai, with the two tablets of the testimony in his hand as he came down from the mountain, Moses did not know that the skin of his face shone because he had been talking with God.

(Exodus 34:29)

The cause of this radiation was a conversation with God. What is interesting to note is that the radiance, although ephemeral, occurred with every talk with God.

Whenever Moses went in before the LORD to speak with him, he would remove the veil, until he came out. And when he came out and told the people of Israel what he was commanded, the people of Israel would see the face of Moses, that the skin of Moses' face was shining. And Moses would put the veil over his face again, until he went in to speak with him.

(Exodus 34:34-35)

The people sought the radiance on the face of Moses. This radiance was a sign to the Israelites that Moses had spoken with God, a visible and physical sign. In the same way, we who contemplate the Lord and have access to His presence can experience this radiance. You can perceive it and it can even be visible to others. When you feel it, focus on God and welcome His presence. God commanded Moses and Aaron to bless the people by saying, «May the Lord make his face shine upon you! «(Numbers 6:25). This blessing is repeated in Psalm 67:

May God be gracious to us and bless us and make his face to shine upon us.

(Psalms 67.1)

This radiance is a blessing, smile, relax and enjoy this sun-bathing of God's love!

The weight of God's glory

When God manifests Himself, we sometimes feel a weight on our hands, on our body. This weight can be so heavy that it is difficult to stand, move around or raise your hands. This is what happened on the day of the inauguration of Solomon's temple. The priests could not bear the presence of God's manifestation and had to leave the Temple.

And when the priests came out of the Holy Place, a cloud filled the house of the LORD, so that the priests could not stand to minister because of the cloud, for the glory of the LORD filled the house of the LORD.

(1 Kings 8:10-11)

The word glory in Hebrew is the word «kabod», it comes from the same root as the word «kabed» which means weight, gravity. It is normal to feel weight when God comes to manifest His glory. I remember a time of prayer when the presence of God was so strong that I couldn't keep my hands up, I felt like I was lifting cast iron, my hands were so heavy! It was after this time in the presence of God that the number of healings in my ministry increased drastically. When you feel God manifesting Himself to you in this way, wait before Him, focus on Him and pray for more. The more time you spend with God, the more glory you will bring to communicate for those around you.

The electricity of the power of the Holy Spirit

Another form of manifestation is to feel electricity in one's body. In the form of discharges, more or less intense shivers, or in continuous waves.

But you will receive power when the Holy Spirit has come upon you, and you will be my witnesses in Jerusalem and in all Judea and Samaria, and to the end of the earth.

(Acts of the Apostles 1.8)

The word «power» used here by Jesus is the Greek word «dunamis» which gave the word dynamo. A dynamo is used to generate electricity. It is normal to feel electricity in your body when the Holy Spirit comes upon you. Some people shake uncontrollably when God comes to touch them. This can be the hand, leg, head, or the whole body. The tremors can vary in intensity until they are very strong.

And he said, "Go out and stand on the mount before the LORD." And behold, the LORD passed by, and a great and strong wind tore the mountains and broke in pieces the rocks before the LORD, but the LORD was not in the wind. And after the wind an earthquake, but the LORD was not in the earthquake. And after the earthquake a fire, but the LORD was not in the fire. And after the fire the sound of a low whisper.

(1 Kings 19:11-12)

When the Almighty passed before Elijah, a strong wind preceded him, tearing the mountains and splitting the rocks in his path. An earthquake and a fire accompanied him! If you experience a manifestation that is on the edge of being bearable, it is because God is not far away. Remain attentive to hear His voice. The fact that our body is the temple of the Holy Spirit and that God has put His power on us without killing us is a miracle in itself. That your body reacts to His power with a tremor should not surprise you.

This list is not exhaustive and when reading the Bible, you will discover what happened during personal encounters between humans and God.

The Peace of God

Concerning emotional manifestations, let us first mention peace. This is what people often feel when they are prayed for, they experience a deep peace that they did not have before prayer. I encourage you to pray softly, without shouting, so that people can receive God's peace more easily. God's peace is beyond our understanding. Jesus slept in the boat in the middle of a storm, for His peace was unshakeable. God's peace can intensify in you as you focus on the Lord's presence. It can be so intense that it causes someone to seem asleep while they are in spiritual rest. The phrase «rest in peace» is often intended for the dead, and many biblical characters were as good as dead when God manifested Himself to them.

When I saw him, I fell at his feet as though dead. But he laid his right hand on me, saying, "Fear not, I am the first and the last.
(Revelation 1:17)

My goal is not to frighten you, but to open your mind to what God is doing, so that you can enjoy what He wants to tell you without being disturbed by theological questions or fears coming from ignorance.

The joy of God

Joy is an emotion that manifests itself in particular through laughter and cries of joy. When it comes to God's joy, it can go beyond the personality of the person experiencing it. A reserved person can burst out laughing when he or she feels God's joy. Remember that on the day of Pentecost, the disciples even seemed drunk.

And all were amazed and perplexed, saying to one another, "What does this mean?" But others mocking said, "They are filled with new wine." But Peter, standing with the eleven, lifted up his voice and addressed them: "Men of Judea and all who dwell in Jerusalem, let this be known to you, and give ear to my words. For these people are not drunk, as you suppose, since it is only the third hour of the day.
(Acts of the Apostles 2:12-15)

Drunken people generally have an unusual and strange behavior. For people to think that the disciples were drunk is because it was obvious to them. Joy is a strength for Christians, and many deprive themselves of it, thinking that God is not joyful. Yet the kingdom of God in our lives is joy!

> *or the kingdom of God is not a matter of eating and drinking but of righteousness and peace and joy in the Holy Spirit.*
>
> *(Romans 14:17)*

Justice and peace should be accompanied by joy. According to this verse, joy represents one third of the kingdom of God! When joy is absent, the Holy Spirit is not fully at work. God is joyful, and His presence communicates joy.

> *Splendor and majesty are before him; strength and joy are in his place.*
>
> *(1 Chronicles 16.27)*

Religious spirits want us to believe that the more God is present, the sadder we have to be. But it's just the opposite! Entering into God's presence is entering into his joy; God is surrounded by joy.

The courage of God

When God comes, he enlivens our hearts. One of the effects is courage or a feeling of inner strength.

> *But you have exalted my horn like that of the wild ox; you have poured over me fresh oil.*
>
> *(Psalms 92.10)*

The consolation of the Holy Spirit

The Holy Spirit is also the Comforter and therefore can comfort us. It is a feeling that settles in us in his presence. Like a child who comes into his/her mother's arms and slowly calms down, while focusing on God, you can let His comfort be communicated to you. Take time to be comforted, it is not instantaneous.

God's Compassion

God can give you His compassion or make you feel His sadness for a situation so that you will intercede. These unpleasant feelings have a purpose: to move you to prayer or action. You need to realize that this is not your sadness, this is not the time to introspect, but to ask God what He wants from you and act accordingly. These feelings should then go away once your prayer has reached its goal.

This list of manifestations is not complete, you will discover by yourself how God manifests Himself to you.

As you stand before God, He will come to manifest Himself to you. You will therefore develop your sensitivity and learn to recognize Him in intimacy. In these moments, welcome the Holy Spirit. For example, saying, «Thank you Holy Spirit for manifesting yourself to me. «Then let him do what He wants to do in you. These intimate times will allow you to recognize His manifestation and He will be able to communicate with you in this way for at least three reasons.

God loves to take his children in his arms, receive his affection.

God can manifest Himself to you at any time: whether you are praying, going about your business, or talking with someone. As you develop sensitivity to the manifestation of

His presence, you will be able to recognize Him, turn your heart to Him in response to His love and receive His affection. When raising your soul to him, when opening your heart to him, his presence will possibly intensify, and you will feel loved and accompanied by God. One of the common languages of love is the language of physical touch. God loves to take his children in his arms like a father who runs his hand through his son's hair to show affection or like a mother who passes by her daughter and kisses her on the forehead. This action has no other purpose than to communicate affection. When God shows you his tenderness, respond, and say «I love you too, Daddy! «Then take time to concentrate on Him inwardly, to increase your awareness of his presence in you and with you.

> *For you did not receive the spirit of slavery to fall back into fear, but you have received the Spirit of adoption as sons, by whom we cry, "Abba! Father!"*
>
> *(Romans 8:15)*

If you have lived in the fear of God until now and the very thought of hearing Him frightens you, begin by presenting yourself to His presence, take baths in His love and let the Holy Spirit in you say, «Daddy (which is the meaning of Abba), I love you! »

God manifests Himself to draw your attention

When God wants to attract your attention, He can speak to you in your thoughts, give you open visions, appear before you, but He especially likes to manifest Himself to you so that by faith you may respond to His invitation.

You have said, "Seek my face." My heart says to you, "Your face, LORD, do I seek."

(Psalms 27.8)

King David felt in his heart that God was drawing him close to him. He recognized that what he felt came from the Lord and he had learned its meaning. That is why he could say in response to this invitation: «I seek your face. «Have you ever felt in your heart that God is drawing you to pray, to read his word, to spend time with him? While learning to recognize God's manifestation, you can allow yourself to be drawn to him in the midst of your life's activities, no matter what the circumstances. When you feel that the Lord is drawing your attention, focus on Him inwardly and ask Him what He wants from you. You may receive a conviction to do something, such as praying for someone, or a warning to protect yourself from making a bad decision, or God may remind you of a Bible verse to guide you, etc.

God also manifests Himself to give us confirmations, for the Holy Spirit bears witness to Jesus

But when the Helper comes, whom I will send to you from the Father, the Spirit of truth, who proceeds from the Father, he will bear witness about me.

(John 15:26)

One of the roles of the Holy Spirit is to bear witness to Jesus and to the truth. This witnessing occurs when the Holy Spirit presses into people's hearts what they have just heard. It is an inner witness, like the disciples on the road to Emmaus. As we saw earlier, their hearts burned when Jesus explained the Scriptures to them. This inner testimony of the Holy Spirit helped them understand and believe what Jesus was teaching and then allowed their eyes to be opened. As you learn to recognize this inner testimony, you can be helped by the Holy Spirit to accept a new thing more easily or to trust more quickly. From one person to another, this witness takes different forms, manifests itself differently, hence the importance of learning to recognize it within your intimacy with God. I'm not saying that this inner witness should supplant your intelligence, your wisdom or what the Bible teaches, but you must take it into account so that you won't limit yourself to what you can understand at first glance or with appearances. The more you pay attention to the inner convictions given by the Holy Spirit, the more sensitive you will be to the absence of His voice. That is to say, you will keep a reserve, which will protect you from liars and temptations. You will thus avoid suffering and loss of time.

Let me tell you this testimony to illustrate my point. I remember a time when Sylvie and I wanted to buy an apartment. We would visit homes, study the market, listen to the real estate agent's advice, plan with the bank, read all kinds of advice on Internet. After a few visits, I realized that I did not feel the testimony of the Holy Spirit in me. I had the impression that he was not with us in this project. His absence challenged me. So I took a time of prayer and while reading the Bible, a verse caught my attention. My conversations with Sylvie about the apartment revolved around the fact that we wanted to build a heritage. The verse that I read that day in the French Courant Bible said that God did not want the Levites to have property when they returned from Babylon, that God himself was their inheritance. Of course, I don't make this a general rule, but I felt in my heart that God was telling me that he didn't want us to buy an apartment. So I decided to trust Him and we stopped our efforts. A few months later, we moved into a house in a housing cooperative, a dwelling more than twice as big for a rent $250 less than our small apartment. God had a plan for us, much better than ours. I rejoice to have listened to the testimony of the Holy Spirit.

God manifests Himself to give you an impulse

There are decisions that require reflection, weighing the implications, calculating. Other decisions are opportunities. For example, you bump into someone and God wants you to tell them about Jesus. This kind of opportunity requires quick choices; you won't have time to pray and fast, read many pages of the Bible, or talk to counselors. Fear, intimidation, or lack of confidence can paralyze you and cause you to miss this opportunity. God may come to you at these times to give you a boost. It is as if he comes to you and says, «Go ahead, trust me, I am with you! «This impulse will give you the courage to take action and take a risk through faith.

In order to be able to follow the directions of the Holy Spirit, you must learn to recognize Him when He manifests Himself to you. You will surely make mistakes a few times, but when accepting to be led by the Holy Spirit, you will also have beautiful experiences that will far surpass your learning errors.

Let us pray together:

Lord, I choose not to limit my relationship with you on an intellectual level. I open my heart to you and ask you to mani-

fest yourself to me. Holy Spirit, instruct me so that I may recognize you when you manifest yourself to me. I ask you to come and touch my life in every way, in the name of Jesus, Amen.

Now I want to pray for you. Prepare to receive a touch of the Holy Spirit.

Father, I now bring to you the fears and misconceptions that have deprived your child of experiencing the manifestation of your presence.

Come Holy Spirit, come and manifest yourself to your child.

I pray that you will saturate his/her heart with your love, that your ever encompassing glory will descend upon him/her now in the name of Jesus.

I pray that the power of the Holy Spirit will flow through His/her body from head to toe.

I pray that you will set his/her heart on fire with your love, that he/ she will know for sure that it is you, like the disciples whose hearts were burning.

Let every cell of his/her body now be sensitive to Your presence. More Lord! Intensify your anointing on him/her in the name of Jesus.

Let your face shine on him/her now.

I pray that you take him/her in your arms and that he/she feels the embrace of your love.

I pray, in the name of Jesus, that you will lead him/her into the wine house and cover him/her with your banner of love. In the name of Jesus, I call God's joy. May his cup overflow! Anoint him/her, Lord, with the oil of joy.

More Lord! Double your anointing on him/her. Thank you, Lord, I bless what you do. Breath, Holy Spirit.

May emotional, intellectual and theological obstacles be overthrown by the manifestation of your presence.

More Lord, more, more in the name of Jesus, Amen.

Now relax, close your eyes for ten minutes, stay focused on Jesus and welcome his presence. I suggest that you do this to music by clicking on the following address:

entdi.eu/piano

«Lord, manifest yourself to me»

You can describe in your journal what you felt.

For God speaks in one way, and in two, though man does not perceive it. In a dream, in a vision of the night, when deep sleep falls on men, while they slumber on their beds, then he opens the ears of men and terrifies them with warnings, that he may turn man aside from his deed and conceal pride from a man; he keeps back his soul from the pit, his life from perishing by the sword.

(Job 33:14-18)

CHAPTER 6.

LISTENING TO GOD IN THE NIGHT

For a long time, I thought that people who had dreams just ate too much pizza. Indeed, the dreams I was told seemed to be meaningless and opposed to my rational mind. But after I began to listen to the voice of God, I experienced for several months a form of harassment from the Holy Spirit to teach about dreams. The problem was that I was not dreaming and had no idea about it. I finally obeyed and began to make a systematic study of dreams and dreams in the Bible. To my surprise, I discovered that this is an important way that God uses to talk to us!

This is what I received from the Lord as I listened to Him in preparing this chapter:

My Spirit is always with you. When you sleep, your mind is more receptive because your thoughts are at rest. Expect me and don't let what I communicate to you fall to the ground.

I draw you closer to me. The dreams I give you pass through the obstacles that prevent you from listening to me when you are awake. I am close to you when you sleep like a mother who watches over her sleeping child and whispers words of love.

The Holy Spirit is always with you; when you sleep, your mind is more receptive, for your thoughts are at rest.

Your mind is one mind with the Spirit of Christ. This union is constant, day and night. At night, God speaks to your spirit through dreams. He wants to give you information, to instruct you, to warn you in order to protect you. When we dream, our intelligence is at rest, but our mind is receptive to what God communicates to us. The story of Solomon is very instructive in this regard.

And the king went to Gibeon to sacrifice there, for that was the great high place. Solomon used to offer a thousand burnt offerings on that altar. At Gibeon the LORD appeared to Solomon in a dream by night, and God said, "Ask what I shall give you." And Solomon said, "You have shown great and steadfast love to your servant David my father, because he walked before you in faithfulness, in righteousness, and in uprightness of heart toward you. And you have kept for him this great and steadfast love and have given him a son to sit on his throne this day. And now, O LORD my God, you have made your servant king in place of David my father, although I am but a little child. I do not know how to go out or come in. And your servant is in the midst of your people whom you have chosen, a great people, too many to be numbered or counted for multitude. Give your servant therefore an understanding mind to govern your people, that I may discern between good and evil, for who is able to govern this your great people?" It pleased the Lord that Solomon had asked this. And God said to him, "Because you have asked this, and have not asked for yourself long life or riches or the life of your enemies, but have asked for yourself understanding to discern what is right, behold, I now do according to your word. Behold, I give you a wise and discerning mind, so that none like you has been before you and none like you shall arise after you. I give you also what you have not asked, both riches and honor, so that no other king shall compare with you, all your days. And if you will walk in my ways, keeping my statutes and my commandments, as your father David walked, then I will lengthen your days." And Solomon awoke, and behold, it was a dream. Then he came to Jerusalem and stood before the ark of the covenant of the Lord, and offered up burnt offerings and peace offerings, and made a feast for all his servants.

(1 Kings 3.4-15)

First of all, notice that it was after offering a thousand sacrifices that Solomon had this dream. Dream and visions are two different translations of the same word. The sacrifices were acts of worship. Cultivate a life of worship to the Lord, raise up his name, offer him the sacrifice of your praise, your time, your fasting, your finances, and stand before him. The more you develop a life of worship before God, the more you can expect to have dreams and visions inspired by God. God appeared to Solomon in a dream and spoke to him. This shows us that God considered Solomon's spirit to be awake. He asked him a question and expected an answer from him. The king, while asleep, answered the Lord. In verse 10, his answer pleased God, who granted him what he had asked for, namely, wisdom and more. So what you say or do in your dreams is important.

Resisting the devil in a dream

Dreams aren't just movies you watch while you're asleep. Sometimes you may be tempted to sin in a dream. It is obviously not the Holy Spirit that tempts you, but the tempter. Just as Solomon was able to respond to God in spirit, you too can resist the temptation presented to you in a dream in the name of Jesus. A woman who discovered this truth shared the following experience with me:

> *I was regularly tempted in my dreams to reach out to men other than my husband. I thought they were just dreams, but it made me uncomfortable and I didn't understand why I was having these dreams. Hearing that I could resist in my dream and not remain passive was a revelation to me. The first time it happened again, I refused this temptation in the name of Jesus and the dream ended! Since then, I have not had a dream like that. Thank you for this revelation that my spirit is awake in my dreams!*

The Bible is clear, Solomon was asleep and woke up, it was a dream (v.15). The story continues with the episode of the two prostitutes who come to see Solomon about one of their sons who died during the night. Solomon then renders justice with supernatural wisdom, proof that God did indeed grant him what he had asked for in his dream.

Receive directions in dreams

The information that God will give you may be guidelines. For example, when Paul dreamed of the Macedonian, the Lord told him where he should continue his mission to proclaim the Gospel.

> *And they went through the region of Phrygia and Galatia, having been forbidden by the Holy Spirit to speak the word in Asia. And when they had come up to Mysia, they attempted to go into Bithynia, but the Spirit of Jesus did not allow them. So, passing by Mysia, they went down to Troas. And a vision appeared to Paul in the night: a man of Macedonia was standing there, urging him and saying, "Come over to Macedonia and help us." And when Paul had seen the vision, immediately we sought to go on into Macedonia, concluding that God had called us to preach the gospel to them.*
>
> *(Acts of the Apostles 16:6-10)*

Paul had made several attempts to travel to Asia and Bithynia. Luke writes that the Spirit of Jesus did not allow them to fulfill their plan. He does not specify how the Holy Spirit opposed this plan, but the apostle recognized the work of the Holy Spirit in this opposition. When Paul had this dream, he concluded that he had to go to Macedonia. This dream was a direction for him, for he had not thought of ministering in that region. This episode in Paul's life shows us that the Holy Spirit speaks in different ways. God-inspired dreams are as valuable as the manifestations, thoughts or visions we receive in prayer. To ignore dreams is to deprive ourselves of important revelations. When you need a revelation or direction, you can pray that God will speak to you through a dream.

Receiving revelations in dreams

God can also give you access to His knowledge, reveal hidden things to you. I often pray for people who are victims of witchcraft. These people often have terrifying nightmares, mysterious dreams in which they find themselves victims of witchcraft rituals. These dreams are in fact words of knowledge. God reveals to them at night what is done against them in the secret of darkness.

> *Each evening they come back, howling like dog sand prowling about the city. There they are, bellowing with their mouths with swords in their lips—for "Who," they think, "will hear us?" But you, O LORD, laugh at them; you hold all the nations in derision. O my Strength, I will watch for you, for you, O God, are my fortress. My God in his steadfast love will meet me; God will let me look in triumph on my enemies. Kill them not, lest my people forget; make them totter by your power and bring them down, O Lord, our shield! For the sin of their mouths, the words of their lips, let them be trapped in their pride. For the cursing and lies that they utter,*
>
> *(Psalms 59:6-12)*

Here the psalmist denounces the work of those who pronounce curses in secret without his knowledge. These curse words are like arrows and swords, but God in his goodness warns him (v.10). In the same way, the Lord can warn you of what is being done against you. You must then undo the words that have been spoken against you and undo the rituals that have been revealed to you, in the name of Jesus.

Let's take the example of someone who has a dream where he is given food and then falls ill. What this person must then do is renounce to this food in the name of Jesus and cancel the words that were spoken against him. Certainly, these dreams are precise instructions for spiritual warfare and deliverance. I will expand on this topic in a future book.

Be warned in dreams

God can also warn you through a dream. The purpose of this warning is to protect you from a danger, a bad decision, an ill-intentioned person. This is what happened to the Magi who came to worship Jesus.

And being warned in a dream not to return to Herod, they departed to their own country by another way.

(Matthew 2:12)

Herod had expressly asked the Magi to tell him where Jesus was so that he too could worship him. Under his noble appearance, Herod was planning a murder. The magi had no idea what he was up to until they had a dream. When God gives you a warning through a dream, it is because your intelligence could not perceive the danger.Let's realize the problems and suffering that could be avoided if Christians heeded God's warnings in dreams. A dream remains a dream, it has no power to change the course of events, it is up to the one who is warned to take the warning seriously and act accordingly to counteract the danger.

Be forewarned in a dream

It also happens that God announces things about the future through a dream. This is what Pharaoh experienced: the dream he had announced the economic future of Egypt for the next fourteen years.

Then Joseph said to Pharaoh, "The dreams of Pharaoh are one; God has revealed to Pharaoh what he is about to do.

(Genesis 41:25)

There will come seven years of great plenty throughout all the land of Egypt, but after them there will arise seven years of famine, and all the plenty will be forgotten in the land of Egypt. The famine will consume the land, and the plenty will be unknown in the land by reason of the famine that will follow, for it will be very severe. And the doubling of Pharaoh's dream means that the thing is fixed by God, and God will shortly bring it about.

(Genesis 41:29-32)

In this case, one should neither pray nor avoid famine, but prepare oneself while stockpiling food, which Joseph did once he was appointed prime minister of Egypt.

You may be wondering how you know what to do after a dream. There are no rules, but one thing is certain: if you take into account the dreams God gives you and learn to interpret them, your life will be more like what God has planned for you and less like what the enemy has planned against you.

The interpretation of dreams is subject to all the principles that govern inspired thoughts and visions, the only difference being that the person is asleep when they receive the revelation. Moreover, dreams can be much more symbolic and mysterious than visions.

Expect God to speak to you at night, even if it seems mysterious.

Although not all dreams are from God, don't be too quick to pass judgment on your dream and reject it, or you may miss a divine message to you. You must believe that this is God's way of speaking and expect to have such an experience.

A good way to express to God your desire that He speak to you at night is to pray like this: «Lord, I entrust my dreams to you, I ask you to speak to me tonight. »

> *In the first year of Belshazzar king of Babylon, Daniel saw a dream and visions of his head as he lay in his bed. Then he wrote down the dream and told the sum of the matter.*
>
> *(Daniel 7:1)*

Just as the prophet Daniel wrote his dream, you too can keep a notebook or something to write in on your bedside table so that you can record your dream as soon as you wake up. Writing down your dream will first help you remember it and read it again later, but it will also make it easier to interpret. Write down all your impressions, the mysterious details, the conviction you had when you woke up, describe the people present, the places, what you felt, what was happening. Indicate whether you were passive or active, what people were saying and anything that caught your attention. This will make it easier for you to interpret the dream. Dreams are sometimes very clear and sometimes very cryptic. Your attitude should go from : «It's just a dream! «to, «Lord, are you talking to me? »

And he said, "Hear my words: If there is a prophet among you, I the LORD make myself known to him in a vision; I speak with him in a dream. Not so with my servant Moses. He is faithful in all my house. With him I speak mouth to mouth, clearly, and not in riddles, and he beholds the form of the LORD. Why then were you not afraid to speak against my servant Moses?"

(Numbers 12:6-8)

Moses had the privilege that God spoke to him without riddles. Since this text states that the Lord will speak to you through riddles, be all the more attentive when a dream is enigmatic. It is possible, for example, that the symbols refer to your personal life. For example, a co-worker may play the simple role of an extra in your dream. This may mean that the dream is related to your work, but not to that particular college. It often happens that people come to me and say, «Pastor, I had a dream, and you were in my dream. Most of the time, this dream has nothing to do with me, but I represent a spiritual authority figure in it. This may mean that it is the Lord speaking to that person. My purpose here is not to give you a list of symbols, because God will use symbols with you that you will understand. Don't be discouraged by the apparent complexity of your dream, but begin to ask the Lord for His interpretation. Joseph and Daniel interpreted dreams, but they did not rely on their intelligence or on a dictionary of symbols. They had first learned to interpret their own dreams before interpreting those of others. But above all, they depended on God to receive interpretations, for God is the author of dreams and he is also the one who reveals their meaning, as Joseph expressed it to the Pharaoh's officials :

> *They said to him, "We have had dreams, and there is no one to interpret them." And Joseph said to them, "Do not interpretations belong to God? Please tell them to me."*
>
> (*Genesis 40:8*)

When you pray, ask God for the overall meaning of the dream or the different parts. God may guide you to the correct interpretation through a more experienced believer. However, since it is your dream, the interpretation must produce an inner conviction in you, just as when God speaks to you in another way. Seek confirmation, take your time and keep your dreams, for the meaning may be revealed to you much later. I recently realized the importance of writing down dreams to keep them.

In March 2014, Guylaine, a Christian from my church in Quebec City, had a dream about me while she was on vacation in Florida. In this dream, I had just moved and I was calling her to ask her questions about taxes. She emailed me the dream with her personal interpretation: «You are going to need help with taxes regarding a past move. «I didn't understand the purpose of the dream and didn't pay attention to it, because I hadn't yet studied the subject of dreams in the Bible, which I did beginning March 2015. Three years later, in March 2017, I told the church committee that I was leaving for Reunion Island. Guylaine was part of the committee and the dream clearly came back to her mind. She found a trace of it in her diary, sent it to me and put me in touch with a tax expert friend who was of a precious help to me for our change of country. I realized that God had given Guylaine this dream three years before we knew we were going to move! The dream did not concern an old move but a new one and after that, I was able to take the right steps with the Quebec administration to organize our departure.

I marvel at the way God speaks. Whether you pay attention or not, he speaks. Don't let go of what He is telling you!

God draws you closer to him, the dreams he gives you pass through the obstacles that prevent you from listening to him when you are awake.

If God uses a dream to speak to us, we must be all the more attentive to the message, because it is information that we could not receive while awake. Remember that God draws your attention through dreams. What you do with them can have important consequences for your life.

When you drive your car, there may be warning lights that indicate certain malfunctions. When you go to a garage, the mechanic, while the car is stationary, can detect problems that you weren't aware of, such as worn drive belts, for example. If you don't replace it and it breaks while you're driving, your engine will be unusable. Disregarding dreams is a bit like ignoring a garage's warnings to maintain your car.

Although there are many different types of dreams, I want to distinguish three categories.

Dreams with a clear message

This is the case, for example, with Joseph's dreams about Jesus.

Now when they had departed, behold, an angel of the Lord appeared to Joseph in a dream and said, "Rise, take the child and his mother, and flee to Egypt, and remain there until I tell you, for Herod is about to search for the child, to destroy him." And he rose and took the child and his mother by night and departed to Egypt.

(Matthew 2:13-14)

This dream is very clear. As soon as he wakes up, Joseph understands the message and obeys it immediately. Joseph's obedience saved Jesus' life. Some dreams may be accompanied by a sense of urgency or strong emotions. It may mean an imperative, as in the case of Joseph and Jesus, but it may also simply be a way for God to challenge you about the importance of the message he is communicating to you without it having an immediate temporal value.

Dreams with a simple interpretation

Some symbols are simple and allow for quick interpretation. This is the case, for example, of Joseph's dreams about his parents and brothers.

Now Joseph had a dream, and when he told it to his brothers they hated him even more. He said to them, "Hear this dream that I have dreamed: Behold, we were binding sheaves in the field, and behold, my sheaf arose and stood upright. And behold, your sheaves gathered around it and bowed down to my sheaf." His brothers said to him, "Are you indeed to reign over us? Or are you indeed to rule over us?" So they hated him even more for his dreams and for his words. Then he dreamed another dream and told it to his brothers and said, "Behold, I have dreamed another dream. Behold, the sun, the moon, and eleven stars were bowing down to me." But when he told it to his father and to his brothers, his father rebuked him and said to him, "What is this dream that

> *you have dreamed? Shall I and your mother and your brothers indeed come to bow ourselves to the ground before you?" And his brothers were jealous of him, but his father kept the saying in mind.*
>
> *(Genesis 37:5-11)*

When hearing the story of Joseph's dream, his brothers and father immediately understood its meaning despite the fact that there were several symbols (the sheaves of wheat, the sun, the moon, the stars, etc.). It is also possible, when you tell a friend about a dream, that the meaning that was hidden from you may seem obvious to him without his needing to pray. We see an example of this with Gideon.

> *When Gideon came, behold, a man was telling a dream to his comrade. And he said, "Behold, I dreamed a dream, and behold, a cake of barley bread tumbled into the camp of Midian and came to the tent and struck it so that it fell and turned it upside down, so that the tent lay flat." And his comrade answered, "This is no other than the sword of Gideon the son of Joash, a man of Israel; God has given into his hand Midian and all the camp." As soon as Gideon heard the telling of the dream and its interpretation, he worshiped. And he returned to the camp of Israel and said, "Arise, for the LORD has given the host of Midian into your hand."*
>
> *(Judges 7:13-15)*

Note here how encouraged Gideon was when he heard the dream and its meaning. Encouragement is also one of God's purposes when He gives us dreams. So be attentive to the dreams that people have about you. In the following passage we see that it was God who urged Gideon to go to the enemy camp to listen to the conversation of two soldiers in order to be strengthened.

> *That same night the LORD said to him, "Arise, go down against the camp, for I have given it into your hand. But if you are afraid to go down, go down to the camp with Purah your servant. And you shall hear what they say, and afterward your hands shall be strengthened to go down against the camp." Then he went down with Purah his servant to the outposts of the armed men who were in the camp.*
>
> *(Judges 7:9-11)*

God could have simply communicated the same message to Gideon, but he wanted Gideon to hear the dream and its meaning. If the Lord chooses to speak to you through a dream, listen to him! Let God choose the method, and receive the message!

It is possible that the person who dreamt about you does not know the meaning of the dream or that their interpretation is wrong, whereas for you the meaning is obvious. Examine the dream and remember what is good!

Some symbols may speak more to some people than to others. Be sure to share your interpretation with one or more spiritual advisors and validate that your interpretation is biblical.

Mysterious dreams

Some dreams require a more advanced and especially more inspired interpretation. Remember that dream interpretation is not a science or an art, but a gift from God. When Pharaoh and Nebuchadnezzar had mysterious dreams, none of the soothsayers, magicians and wise men in their courts could interpret them, for the interpretation of dreams belongs to God.

> *And Daniel went in and requested the king to appoint him a time, that he might show the interpretation to the king. Then Daniel went to his house and made the matter known to Hananiah, Mishael, and Azariah, his companions, and told them to seek mercy from the God of heaven concerning this mystery, so that Daniel and his companions might not be destroyed with the rest of the wise men of Babylon. Then the mystery was revealed to Daniel in a vision of the night. Then Daniel blessed the God of heaven.*
>
> *(Daniel 2:16-19)*

Enigmatic dreams push us to seek interpretation from God. The curiosity and emotions aroused by mysterious dreams produce a strong desire to implore God in order to receive their meaning. The Lord can thus dialogue with us on a subject that we would not normally consider. Notice that Daniel received the interpretation in a vision during the night, it was not the fruit of a study or a great personal analysis.

If you look at Joseph's life, you will see that the dreams he interpreted became more and more complex. So I encourage you to persevere in writing down your dreams and interpreting them. You will find over time that God will increase the number of your dreams as well as their scope.

> *They said to him, "We have had dreams, and there is no one to interpret them." And Joseph said to them, "Do not interpretations belong to God? Please tell them to me."*
>
> *(Genesis 40:8)*

You'll always be an apprentice. God will give you experiences that will be used to help others, like Joseph who had dreams and was used many times to interpret other people's dreams.

God is near you when you sleep, like a mother who watches over her sleeping child and whispers words of love to him

bless the LORD who gives me counsel; in the night also my heart instructs me.

(Psalms 16.7)

Most of your dreams will be about your personal life. The Lord indeed gives you dreams about your life to accompany you on your spiritual journey. Others, on the contrary, are about external situations. Most of the time, these kinds of dreams are meant to lead us to intercession or to communicate a message to someone. Isn't it wonderful to know that God is so close to us, that he advises us, that he encourages us even when we sleep?

I invite you to pray with me:

Lord, I offer you my nights and I beg you to purify my dreams. I choose to believe that you want to talk to me at night too. I expect you to instruct me,to advise me, to counsel me,to encourage me,to reveal hidden things to me, I ask this in the name of Jesus, Amen.

Consider the following passage of Scripture:

As for these four youths, God gave them learning and skill in all literature and wisdom, and Daniel had understanding in all visions and dreams.

(Daniel 1:17)

Because God gave Daniel the gift of interpreting dreams and visions, I am going to pray for you now so that you too can interpret the dreams, yours, those of the believers around you, and those of the people who are called to meet the author of the dreams.

Father, I pray in the name of Jesus that you grant your child dreams and visions. I pray that you now cleanse his/her thoughts and that his/her nights are peaceful so that he/she can hear your whisper in his/her ear. I ask you to exhort, counsel, instruct and warn him/her, and to reveal to him/her things hidden in the night. In the name of Jesus, I pray that you grant him/her the gift of interpreting dreams and a deposit of faith and wisdom so that he/she will know what to do with the dreams he/she has. I pray that you will lead your child to your school, Holy Spirit, that he/she will make progress and grow, that he/she will be introduced to those who dream but do not understand their dreams. Lead him/her to the courts of kings, in the name of Jesus, Amen.

Practice exercise

Now it's time to put into practice what you've just read! Relax physically and mentally and take notes. Play some instrumental music, for example click on the following address:

entdi.eu/piano

Focus your attention on Jesus and then say:

«Lord, here I am, speak, your child is listening. »

Stay focused on Jesus in you and then write down what comes spontaneously into your mind (thought, image). Do not try to analyze while you are receiving. Remain in simple faith, just like a child, while you receive. Once you have finished (give yourself time, at least ten minutes), examine what you have received. Focus on the Holy Spirit within you and write one of the following questions in your journal:

«What do you want to tell me today? »

«What do you want to tell me about my dreams? »

If you have had a dream recently, write it down in your journal and ask God what it means.

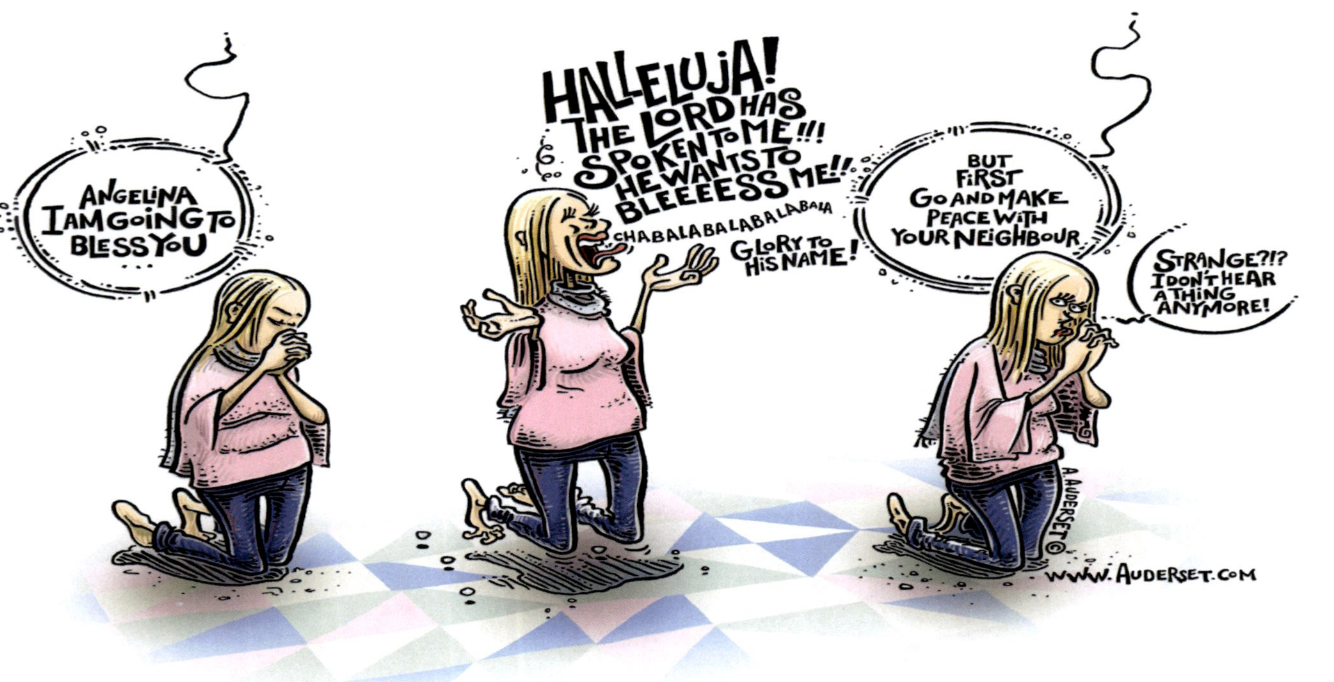
ANGELINA I AM GOING TO BLESS YOU ...
HALLELUJA! THE LORD HAS SPOKEN TO ME!!! HE WANTS TO BLEEEEESS ME!!
CHABALABALABALABALA
GLORY TO HIS NAME!
BUT FIRST GO AND MAKE PEACE WITH YOUR NEIGHBOUR
STRANGE?!? I DON'T HEAR A THING ANYMORE!
A. AUDERSET ©
WWW. AUDERSET.COM

CHAPTER 7

RECEIVING THE KEYS OF HEARTS

To each is given the manifestation of the Spirit for the common good. For to one is given through the Spirit the utterance of wisdom, and to another the utterance of knowledge according to the same Spirit.

(1 Corinthians 12:7-8)

These are the things I received from the Lord as I listened to him in preparing this chapter:

I am God, I know everything and I demonstrate my love, power and care for each of my children. Draw from my knowledge to open hearts. I have the key to every door, to every heart. I want to reveal mysteries and secrets in my intimacy.

The word of knowledge is one of the ways in which God demonstrates His love and care for His children.

The Holy Spirit, who lives in you, is God. He is omniscient, which means that He knows everything, really everything, about you and everyone else. Psalm 139 shows us how intimate and precise God's knowledge of us is:

O LORD, you have searched me and known me!

(Psalms 139.1)

The Holy Spirit knows what is in the depths of your heart, your aspirations, your dreams, your wounds, the deficiencies and lacks you have faced in your life and so much more. He knows everything. He knows what you are going to say before the word comes out of your mouth. He knows what you are thinking, every moment. Not only does he know all this information about you, but he also knows everyone around you, those who belong to him and those who still live far away from him.

God is not a secret database that collects information about humans. He is a loving father who wants to adopt his children who are still outside his kingdom. He uses his omniscience to draw all men to himself. This is what Jesus said through this verse:

And I, when I am lifted up from the earth, will draw all people to myself."

(John 12:32)

The Lord does not use what He knows about us as a hurtful harpoon to catch us. On the contrary, words of knowledge act as chains of love, human bonds.

I led them with cords of kindness, with the bands of love.

(Hosea 11:4)

God uses His children (you and me) by sharing His knowledge with them to show His care for those who do not yet belong to Him. When someone takes care to give you a gift that suits your particular taste, it is a gesture that means: «I love you". When the Lord shows that he knows you intimately, he proves to you that he is close to you and interested in you. The fact that He knows your secrets and shows it to you through someone else who has a word of knowledge produces wonder in you. You say to yourself: «God is real and He really knows everything! »

The word of knowledge most frequently manifests itself unconsciously in prayer. Someone prays and his or her prayer seems to respond precisely to the secret aspirations of the person receiving the prayer. It is in fact the Holy Spirit who has inspired prayer to demonstrate that God hears the sighs of his child's heart. People then say something like, «Your prayer touched me very much,» or, «That's exactly what I needed to hear". The person is blessed not by the answer to the prayer, but by the content of the prayer. If you have ever been told this after a prayer, it is probably because you have practiced the word of knowledge without knowing it.

God wants to use you more, more precisely, more frequently and consciously. If you willingly listen to Him and ask Him to give you words of knowledge, you will exercise your faith, and the Lord will give you secret information supernaturally through the Holy Spirit.

For to one is given through the Spirit the utterance of wisdom, and to another the utterance of knowledge according to the same Spirit.

(1 Corinthians 12:8)

A word of knowledge is information that God communicates to you by His Spirit and which must be shared, declared in order to accomplish His purpose. You can receive this information in different ways. First, it can be in the form of an inspired thought, whether in a moment of personal prayer or spontaneously in a conversation or during a time of prayer with someone.

As I prayed for the business of a fellow Christian whose business was going badly, the thought came to me: «Do you have a partner? «I was convinced that this Christian was working alone. Recognizing that this thought might be coming from the Holy Spirit, I asked him the question. He replied, «Yes, I have a partner, and he is a Free Mason. «God had just brought to light the source of this Christian's problems. He had partnered with a man who served the darkness. I gave him some advice, and after praying, he decided to break up with his business partner. He then regained the inner peace he had lost, and God blessed him with a better job, better hours, and better pay.

When you spontaneously think (or after having asked God for it) of information that was unknown to you, dare to ask the question by faith to the person you are speaking to, it is perhaps a word of knowledge, the key to unblock a situation or open a heart.

One day when I was praying for the people who had responded to a call to the altar after a sermon, God told me, «This man is an orphan. «This information had to be treated with care, for it brings us to a holy land, the heart of the person's heart. So I asked him, «Did you know your father? This man in his fifties answered, «He died when I was two years old. «I asked him if I could pray for him to experience God's love as a Father. He said yes, and I took him in my arms. Here is Daniel Niambi's testimony:

Great was my astonishment to hear the pastor ask me from the beginning if I had a good relationship with my biological father. I simply replied that I didn't really know him, since he died when I was less than two years old and I only have three vague and rather painful memories of him. So I didn't know any fatherly love. Having received permission from me to hug me like a father would, the pastor hugged me while he transmitted the following prophetic word: «Open your heart and let the Holy Spirit flood it. You have a good heart and God loves it. The Lord has given you a spirit of compassion, of adopting His children who feel lonely, abandoned, forsaken, orphaned. You will come to their aid to bring them back to the Lord our God. Say DAD to the Lord, say DAD often. Psalm 27:10, which says, «Even though my father and mother forsake me, the LORD will take me in», will be your psalm from now on. «After that, he prayed for me that I might regain inner peace and taste the consolation of the Eternal Father. From that day on, the emptiness that I constantly felt within me was filled by the presence and love of my heavenly Father. I feel His peace and I have learned to address Him as if I were addressing a biological father, created in His image. I feel closer to him and day after day a great complicity develops between him and me. From now on, I know that I can simply talk to him, present my needs to him, ask him questions, intercede for others and expect him, in the name of Jesus, just as a son would do with his biological father. I am often amazed at the ways he responds to me: visions, dreams, , revelations, words of knowledge or wisdom, and many other riddles. All this makes me thirsty to constantly seek him, to fear him, to obey him and to grow in his presence. As I often address my requests to the Eternal Father in the name of Jesus, it is above all from Jesus that I receive the Father's answers. I had lost an earthly fatherly love; I have gained the love of my heavenly Father who created me. I am gradually learning to walk with him to enter into my destiny by serving him. Thank you for everything, Eternal Father!

If God gives you a key, it is not to start a collection, but to open the locks of the chains that imprison hearts.

"The Spirit of the Lord is upon me because he has anointed me to proclaim good news to the poor. He has sent me to proclaim liberty to the captives and recovering of sight to the blind, to set at liberty those who are oppressed, to proclaim the year of the Lord's favor."

(Luke 4:18-19)

So if God reveals something negative to you, it is so that you pray for freedom or blessing.

It is also possible to feel what God reveals to us, whether in physical or emotional form. For example, you may feel someone's suffering or emotions. You need to be attentive to what you are feeling in order to be able to distinguish your own pain or emotions from a spontaneous emotion that comes over you or a sudden affliction whose origin you do not understand. If the Lord shows you someone's suffering or sadness, it is because He wants you to pray for the person to be comforted or healed. Personally, I very often feel the physical pain of the people around me. This is an opportunity to pray for healing. I don't necessarily know who is in pain, but by asking questions around me, I end up finding out who to pray for.

The phrase " word of knowledge "contains the word ''word" because it must be expressed and not preserved internally.

During a discussion with a representative at the office, I felt a lot of pain in my knee. Realizing that it was not my pain, but the representative's, I examined her posture. She did not express any grin of pain, nor did she limp. Thinking I was wrong, I greeted her and let her go. After she left my office, I felt my heart beating more strongly, and I understood that the Holy Spirit was urging me to share this word of knowledge despite appearances. So I ran after her and asked, «Can I ask you a question? Do you have a sore knee?» She immediately had tears in her eyes and answered, «How do you know that? I have pain every night and it keeps me awake, how did you guess? «I replied that I was practicing listening to God and that he had made me feel her pain to show her in a concrete way that He knew her perfectly, that He had compassion for her and that he wanted to heal her. I then suggested to this lady to pray for her and let her go. She came back a week later with documents and told me that the pain had diminished. I prayed for her again and told her about God's love. I never thought she would be so open to hearing about God.

This word of knowledge was the key that gave me access to her heart to tell her about the Lord.

People feel loved when they realize that God knows their personal suffering. The Lord stands close to the one who suffers, He has compassion on him / her.

The LORD is near to the brokenhearted and saves the crushed in spirit.

(Psalms 34:18)

One day when I was at the restaurant with Sylvie, I felt the Holy Spirit drawing my attention to an elderly lady who was eating alone two tables away from us. I decided to go and talk to her and asked her if she had pain in her body. She replied, «Will you heal me? Do you have a gift?» I explained to her that I was praying in the name of Jesus. She added that she had prayed that very morning and asked God to send someone to her, because she could no longer bear to suffer. I had the opportunity to pray with her before she left the restaurant.

God can reveal to you the secret prayers of hearts. If you use them to communicate His love to people, He will give you more. In fact, there is no limit to what God knows, or what He can reveal to you as a type of information.

I was talking to a programmer at the restaurant about a website. He had been trying to solve a bug on his site for more than two days. I mentioned to him that God can work miracles in any field and that taking time to listen to him was precious. I explained that «wasting time» to listen to the Lord can actually save us a lot of time! During the meal, a colleague of this programmer received two numbers in his mind. He is a graphic designer and therefore knows nothing about programming.

At the end of the evening, the programmer decided to spend the night at the office to find the error. The graphic designer, who had received the two numbers, shared them with him as he left the restaurant, not knowing what the two numbers corresponded to. Upon arriving at the office, the programmer reread the lines of code corresponding to the two numbers and noticed, on one of these lines, the programming error. Within five minutes, the bug was fixed. The file contained nearly 200 lines of code, but the Lord had revealed exactly where the source of the problem was.

Draw on the knowledge of God to open hearts; the Lord has the key to every door, to every heart.

A word of knowledge can be used to open a closed heart so that the heart is then willing to meet God.

Philip found Nathanael and said to him, "We have found him of whom Moses in the Law and also the prophets wrote, Jesus of Nazareth, the son of Joseph." Nathanael said to him, "Can anything good come out of Nazareth?" Philip said to him, "Come and see." Jesus saw Nathanael coming toward him and said of him, "Behold, an Israelite indeed, in whom there is no deceit!" Nathanael said to him, "How do you know me?" Jesus answered him, "Before Philip called you, when you were under the fig tree, I saw you." Nathanael answered him, "Rabbi, you are the Son of God! You are the King of Israel!"

(John 1.45-49)

Have you ever wanted to testify about Jesus to someone whose heart is closed? This kind of heart seems insensitive to arguments; it is like a locked heart. Rather than trying to use all the keys you have, ask God, who knows the person perfectly, to give you the key to his or her heart.

In spite of Philip's testimony, Nathaniel was very skeptical about Jesus. Intellectual obstacles prevented him from conceiving that Jesus could be the Messiah of Israel. When Jesus met him, he gave Nathaniel two words of knowledge. The first was to reveal the purity of his heart, the second was a demonstration of God's omniscience. Remember that the words of knowledge are like chains of love to draw people to the Lord. When telling Nathaniel that his heart was pure and upright, Jesus honored him. Words of knowledge are a way to show love to someone. When you tell a person on behalf of God what is good in them, they feel loved. It may seem trivial to you, but telling a man, for example, that he is a good father can produce a powerful encouragement in him and open his heart to receive more from God. What, you may ask, is the difference between a simple encouragement and a word of knowledge? The word of knowledge will reveal precisely the aspiration, the motivation of the person's heart. If you, too, want to receive specific information such as addresses or names, agree to begin sharing in a loving way the simple things that God reveals to you. Nathaniel's response, «Where do you know me from?» shows how moved he was that Jesus knew the depths of his heart. It was as if, at that moment, Jesus had entered the key into the lock of his heart. Then we see that Jesus uses the second word of knowledge as a key turn that opens the lock.

Jesus said to Nathaniel, «I saw you under the fig tree. «First of all, understand here that Jesus did not physically see Nathaniel under the fig tree. Jesus had a vision in which he saw him under the tree. The text does not tell us what this man was doing there. Perhaps he was praying, talking to God or asking for forgiveness. But one thing is certain, what he was doing under the fig tree must have been important, because this one piece of information revealed by Jesus was enough to make him change his mind. While he was skeptical about Jesus, he suddenly recognized that Jesus was the Son of God, the King of Israel. These titles are extremely strong in the mouth of a Jew, they were declared right after this simple statement: «I saw you under the fig tree. »

One day, I was praying with Sylvie for a woman (whom I will name Esther) who had been sexually abused. At the end of the prayer, I declared that God was giving Esther a robe of purity and honor instead of the robe of shame and defilement that she had been wearing for many years. Then I heard in my mind that it was a fragrant dress, that it gave off a scent with every movement and that others around could smell the fragrance. At the time, I thought for a few moments about the relevance of releasing this word. Since the Bible says that we spread the good odor of the knowledge of Christ, I found that it was biblical and that it could do no harm, so by faith I declared it in my prayer. Esther then began to cry harder. At the end of my prayer, once I had calmed down, Esther told us that what had touched her the most was that the dress was perfumed, because she had grown up on a farm and was haunted by the smell of the barn when she arrived at school. As a young girl, she had been mocked by the students in her class about it. I had no idea what the problem was. The Lord knew and had just healed her wounds.

God can reveal a person's past, present, concerns, circumstances, thoughts, prayers, aspirations, and desires of the heart. The goal is to show him that he knows him and to attract him to himself through his love.

Remember that the word of knowledge is a demonstration of God's love.

It can happen that the Lord reveals information to us about a problem in someone's life. This is the case of Jesus with the Samaritan woman at Jacob's well in chapter four of John's Gospel. Here is the end of the conversation:

> *Jesus said to her, "Go, call your husband, and come here." The woman answered him, "I have no husband." Jesus said to her, "You are right in saying, 'I have no husband'; for you have had five husbands, and the one you now have is not your husband. What you have said is true."*
>
> *(John 4:16-18)*

It is important to keep in mind that God's intention is to draw the person to Himself through His goodness and love. The information he reveals to you must therefore be used for this purpose. Remember that the Lord knew the information before He revealed it to you and that the person also knows his problem. Telling them will not solve their problem, nor will the fact that they know that God has revealed it to you. So let's look together at how Jesus used this word of knowledge.

Let us note that Jesus first offered the Samaritan woman living water to quench her thirst and make her a spring. It was only when she asked for this water that Jesus asked her to call her husband. The Samaritan woman answered honestly and Jesus confirmed her honesty by telling her that she had had five husbands. At this point, Jesus showed this woman that He knew very well who He was talking to, that her marital situation did not prevent Him from offering her this living water. The Samaritan woman then experiences the grace of God. We see here that Jesus used the knowledge he had of this woman's life to make her feel loved unconditionally. In the same way, we must call people to come closer to God, so let us be careful not to use what the Lord reveals to us to push people away, but to draw them to Him. Ask the Holy Spirit to show you how to use what He reveals to you in the best way, and follow His instructions without haste.

God wants to reveal mysteries and secrets to you in his intimacy.

Jesus spoke in parables and privately explained their meaning to his disciples. When we come into the intimacy of Jesus, when we listen to him, he reveals his secrets to us.

The friendship of the LORD is for those who fear him, and he makes known to them his covenant.

(Psalms 25:14)

God has secrets He wants to reveal to you. The things of the Spirit are both simple and profound. The Bible speaks of powerful spiritual realities in very simple pictorial language. Intelligence cannot grasp these truths without the Holy Spirit revealing them.

But we impart a secret and hidden wisdom of God, which God decreed before the ages for our glory. None of the rulers of this age understood this, for if they had, they would not have crucified the Lord of glory. But, as it is written "What no eye has seen, nor ear heard,

> *nor the heart of man imagined, what God has prepared for those who love him"—these things God has revealed to us through the Spirit. For the Spirit searches everything, even the depths of God. For who knows a person's thoughts except the spirit of that person, which is in him? So also no one comprehends the thoughts of God except the Spirit of God. Now we have received not the spirit of the world, but the Spirit who is from God, that we might understand the things freely given us by God.*
>
> *(1 Corinthians 2:7-12)*

God's secrets have been prepared for us. What God wants is to reveal them to us. A bit like a father who organizes a treasure hunt for his children. The purpose of the activity is for the children to find the treasure, to be happy and to enjoy it. When we spend time listening to God, he reveals his mysteries to us. Regularly, God opens my eyes to spiritual principles that I had not yet grasped, even though I had read them several times in the Bible. These revelations then become treasures when I put them into practice. Most of the time I am surprised when I receive these kinds of revelations, because I didn't expect them. I am simply listening to God, and He is speaking to me. Then I study what the Bible says about it and I see things from a new perspective, the revelation becomes a new reality for me. It is difficult for faith to rely on information. Faith is actually based on revelations. You can receive these revelations in the form of images in a vision, in the form of a dialogue with God, or in the form of a dream. You can also ask the Lord to explain to you a concept or verse that you do not understand or whose significance you do not grasp. Revelation will allow you to make this spiritual reality your own. Spend time in the intimacy of God and He will reveal His mysteries to you. You will then be able to share them to those around you so that others can benefit from them. What revelation does God want to grant you today? Take time in his presence and listen to him!

I invite you to pray with me.

Father, I recognize today that I need you, for my knowledge is limited. Thank you for the gift of the word of knowledge. I decide to draw from your resources in order to receive keys, treasures, revelations. Give me your love, wisdom and faith to use the keys you give me and free the captives. Holy Spirit, teach me the things of the Spirit and reveal to me the things that God has given me by His grace, in the name of Jesus, Amen.

I will pray for you now. Read the following prayer and then take a few minutes of silence before God to let Him work in you.

Father, You know all things, and the Holy Spirit distributes the words of knowledge. I pray that you will give your child access to your resources of knowledge to lead him/her, and make him/her a magnet that draws people to you. Thank you for making him/her thirsty to receive information from you that will enable him/her to pray effectively. I pray for a deposit of faith so that he/she will use what you communicate to him/her and for a blanket of love so that people will feel loved. May words of knowledge abound in his/her life, through thoughts, impressions, visions, dreams, feelings. May people be amazed, may hearts open and may all the glory return to you, in the name of Jesus, Amen.

Practice exercise

Now it's time to put into practice what you've just read! Relax physically and mentally and take notes. Play some instrumental music, for example click on the following address:

entdi.eu / piano

Focus on the Holy Spirit within you and write the following question:

«Lord, what do you want to reveal to me? »

Depending on what you have received, ask questions to God about what you should do with this revelation. Write down what he has answered you.

Ask God to tell you who needs prayer and what their need is.

Then contact this person and pray for them, asking if your prayer reaches them. Note his or her reaction in your diary.

CHAPTER 8

CONSERVING HIS WORDS

Now these things happened to them as an example, but they were written down for our instruction, on whom the end of the ages has come.

(1 Corinthians 10:11)

The more time you spend listening to God, the more your ability to hear him will develop. You will therefore have to digest the revelations that the Lord has given you. In my personal life, the amount of revelations He gives me is more than I can absorb, so I need to regularly reread what He has told me to make it my own. It would be impossible for me to remember precisely everything I received if I did not write it down.

If we have the Bible in our hands, it is because it has been written down. Not only the history of God's men and women, but also what God has said to them, has been written for our instruction.

The Word of God cannot have an effect in our hearts if we have forgotten it or if we no longer have access to it. The very fact of writing down what we receive makes it easier to remember. The king of Israel was instructed at the beginning of his reign to copy the law of God himself into a book and then to meditate on it daily (De 17:18). This is what I received in preparing this chapter:

Do not drop my words on the ground. Take time to examine what you receive, hold on to what is good and hold it in your heart. Rely on my words to move forward, my words are food for your soul, don't let the bread I give you be stolen. You will need to meditate on what I am telling you so that your thoughts can be changed. Keep them preciously as love letters.

Don't let his words fall to the ground

And Samuel grew, and the LORD was with him and let none of his words fall to the ground.

(1 Samuel 3:19)

When God first manifested Himself to Samuel, He called him by his first name. But the young servant had a share in all the revelations God wanted to give him when he actually listened to him. Scripture mentions that Samuel addressed the Lord like this: «Speak, O LORD, your servant is listening. «We see that God caught Samuel's attention by calling him by his first name, but did not reveal his message to him until the young boy showed him that he had his full attention. Saying to God, «I am here to listen to you,» is a good way to begin a listening time. Beyond our words, the Lord knows our hearts; indeed, we can repeat this phrase as a formula without being willing to listen. Taking notes allows us to involve our body (our hands and eyes), our intelligence (to transcribe what we receive) and shows God that we will not let his words fall to the ground.

Being prepared to take notes is also a demonstration of faith. I am proving that I expect God to speak to me. It is faith that pleases the Lord, and He rewards it. As you prepare to take notes, you cannot know what the content of your dialogue with God will be. Will it be encouragement, a powerful revelation, a precise directive for the day or for a person, a direction for your destiny, a mysterious vision in several parts? Do not make the mistake of believing that you will remember everything He has told you.

This advice also applies to words you receive through someone else. Record or write down what you have received right away, so that you can quietly review it later and sometimes read it again years later for encouragement.

The Lord is looking for men and women who thirst for His words and who will treasure them. I truly believe that by recording what you receive from God, you are preparing to receive more. He who is faithful in little things will receive more (Mt 25:21).

Take the time to examine what you receive, remember what is good.

Do not despise prophecies, but test everything; hold fast what is good.

(1 Thessalonians 5:20-21)

When God speaks to us or we think that he speaks to us, we may be excited or perplexed and have difficulty filtering out what comes from God and what may come from our thoughts. Remember that the Lord also speaks through symbols and riddles. Add to this the fact that His thoughts may oppose your own thoughts and engage your faith. All these reasons show how important it is to write down what you receive from God so that you can then examine it.

The apostle Paul mentions that we should not despise the inspired messages. If he mentions this, it is because we can easily despise, neglect, or drop to the ground what God is telling us for the reasons I mentioned earlier. Paul continues his exhortation by telling us to examine all things. Before talking about examination, what does he mean by all things? Well, really everything!

This implies that we keep a written record of everything we receive: thoughts, images, impressions, deep convictions, paths traced in our hearts, dreams, divine or angelic encounters. When we understand that it is possible to despise a word that comes from God, we become attentive to the slightest whisper from him. We are like treasure hunters who must not neglect any clue. I also want to mention that God is creative, he can use many forms of communication. Some will be familiar to us, but others will be unknown to us. So, even if it seems strange to you, please take time to write before examining what you have received and don't be too quick to reject unusual things.

You must know that God can use your five spiritual senses (sight, hearing, touch, smell, and taste) to get your attention. For example, it is possible that the Lord may give you a scent to communicate a message to you. He may also use whatever you can understand, which may include the lyrics of songs you know or the pictures from movies you have seen. God can use a variety of means to speak to you. So I recommend that you take the following steps:

1. Set yourself up to listen to Him

2. Write in as much detail as possible what you received (describe your vision, your dream, what you felt, write down every word you heard).

3. Examine what you have received in the light of the Bible and your knowledge of God.

4. Ask the Lord additional questions to understand the meaning of what you have received or to get more details.

5. Talk to a spiritual counselor who hears God's voice.

Do not despise prophecies, but test everything; hold fast what is good.

(1 Thessalonians 5:20-21)

Notice that the Apostle Paul uses an imperative. It is our responsibility to examine all things. Whether it is something reasonable and logical, or whether it is something strange and unexpected, whether you received it personally or someone else communicated it to you. It also implies that you must examine what is shared with you, regardless of the messenger. Too many disappointments occur when believers rely on the messenger's reputation and neglect the process of examination. Conversely, there are also times when the messenger (i.e., the person who shares the word with us) is mistreated by us and the message is rejected.

The context of Paul's warning is that of public prophecy. But if you want to be able to examine public prophecy, you must first learn to examine what you personally receive.

The word «examine» is also translated as «to test, to expirement, to verify» and also has the meaning of «to probe, to validate». This examination requires the use of our intelligence. Our intelligence is at rest when we pray in the Spirit and listen to God, but we must use it to examine what we have received.

For if I pray in a tongue, my spirit prays but my mind is unfruitful.
(1 Corinthians 14:14)

Here are a few questions you can use to examine:

- ·Is it biblical?
- ·Was it a thought or a spontaneous image?
- ·Were my eyes on Jesus or was I just thinking?
- ·Does this correspond to the nature and character of God?
- ·What does it produce in me?
- ·What has God ever told me about this?
- ·Does this confirm what I received previously, or do I need confirmations?

It is not a lack of faith to want to examine what one has received, it is a proof of maturity. Of course, it is not necessary for this examination to last for years, but if you want God to entrust you with more, you must prove to Him that you are trustworthy and that you do not believe everything that comes into your head or everything that is told to you.

Remember what's good

When we learn to listen to God, we make mistakes. We may confuse our thoughts with God's thoughts or misinterpret them. The good news is that it is possible to retain something good even when we make a mistake. Someone said, «Eat the chicken and spit out the bones! ».

Also don't believe the lie that very experienced people don't get it wrong anymore.

Having gifts that differ according to the grace given to us, let us use them: if prophecy, in proportion to our faith.

(Romans 12.6)

No matter what our level of experience, we prophesy by faith, and the Apostle Paul's command is still valid: «Examine ALL THINGS. »

Remember what is good, but write it all down, as your ability to examine will develop as you keep practicing. If your review does not allow you to reach a conclusion, don't worry. If it is important, God will tell you about it somehow. Then you will remember that this is not the first time he has drawn your attention to this subject. The elements added together will certainly give you a better understanding.

It often happens that God speaks as if in the form of a puzzle. He gives us pieces as he goes along. The scope is not always known to us when we receive the first piece. But when we have all the pieces, the meaning becomes obvious.

It may also happen that, out of unbelief, you reject something that came from God. When you read your notes later, you will find that you heard the Lord speaking to you and your faith will grow.

A friend was at a restaurant counter and as she was using the payment terminal, she heard clearly in her mind, «His name is Jason». At first she thought it was ridiculous, that God couldn't give her the cashier's name, that it must be her own thoughts. After she finished entering her credit card code, she looked up and was surprised to see that the cashier was wearing a name tag with his first name, «Jason». This was an opportunity for her to «test» that it was God speaking to her and that she could expect this level of accuracy in words of knowledge.

Hold his words in your heart,
lean on them to grow in your faith.

Once you have examined what you have received and retained what is good, remember that God's word is alive and is a support for your faith.

This charge I entrust to you, Timothy, my child, in accordance with the prophecies previously made about you, that by them you may wage the good warfare.

(1 Timothy 1:18)

God does not speak just for the sake of a spiritual experience. His words are useful in our lives. If we neglect God's words, we will not be able to rely on them in our later struggles. Could it be that many battles will be lost for lack of strength because God's encouragement has been despised and forgotten?

We tend to seek encouragement when we are distressed. Yet our anxious state of mind in difficult circumstances can diminish our ability to hear God. If we have regularly taken time to listen to God and have written down His words, it will be easy for us, regardless of our emotions, to reread our journal and build on what He has told us previously, which will then be a source of supernatural strength. The Lord knows in advance the battles you will have to fight. He can therefore encourage you before the battle begins, when the dispositions of your heart make you more receptive to His voice.

I regularly re-read several months or even a whole year's worth of my diary, and each time it is a great source of encouragement. By rereading at once what I have received over several months, I often see a theme or a thread that I hadn't noticed on a day-to-day basis.

It also allows me to realize that God had begun to challenge me on a subject months before I finally understood what he meant.

Often the Lord will give us advice, inspired ideas or ask us to do something. We can easily forget what he has told us, as the concerns of daily life accumulate in our thoughts. By re-reading what he has shared with us, we can keep our attention on what he is asking of us. So, instead of waiting for God to repeat what he has already asked you, read what he has already told you, you will save time! If you realize that you have been negligent, disobedient or lacked faith, simply ask for forgiveness and start over where you left off.

Some words are announcements of what God is going to do, promises. Circumstances will often conflict with them, which is why the Lord reveals to you in advance what He will do. In order to remain in faith and to live up to His promises, you too, like Mary, will have to hold God's words close to your heart.

But Mary treasured up all these things, pondering them in her heart.

(Luke 2:19)

God does not have the same notion of time as we do. He will sometimes let you know something that will seem far away, but it is for a very near future. Other times, he will communicate his thoughts to you with such emotional intensity that you will be tempted to believe it is imminent. If the Lord leaves a strong impression on your heart, it doesn't necessarily mean that it is for now, but rather that He wants to make sure that He has your attention and that it is engraved in your memory. Don't be discouraged if you make a misinterpretation over time. I advise you not to look for precise dates, because very few biblical prophecies contain them. However, it is possible that God will give you a date, but be careful to avoid unfortunate consequences if you make a mistake.

However, there will be many situations where you will have nothing to write about and what you will receive from God for someone or for a particular action will be for the present. Then, because you will have become accustomed to recognizing His voice, you will have to go through a process of quick inner examination and then act by faith. Writing what you receive from God is therefore also a training and a springboard for action.

The words of God are food for your soul, do not let the bread that God gives you be stolen.

The first time God spoke to me in my thoughts, I felt full. When I neglect to listen for a few days, I feel that my soul is hungry to hear him.

But he answered, "It is written, "'Man shall not live by bread alone, but by every word that comes from the mouth of God.

(Matthew 4.4)

Jesus did not say of every word that came out of the mouth of God, but that goes out. It is in the present tense. What the Lord says today is food for my soul, whether it is a verse that the Holy Spirit illuminates in my heart or a revelation in spirit. If I am to be nourished by what comes out of God's mouth, then how can I be strengthened without listening to Him? To live without dialogue with God is to expose myself to weakness and make me vulnerable to the enemy. This is why the enemy makes Christians believe that God no longer speaks and thus steals from them what they receive from their heavenly Father.

And as he sowed, some seeds fell along the path, and the birds came and devoured them

(Matthew 13.4)

"Hear then the parable of the sower: When anyone hears the word of the kingdom and does not understand it, the evil one comes and snatches away what has been sown in his heart. This is what was sown along the path.

(Matthew 13:18-19)

These verses are not exclusively reserved for salvation. Jesus uses the expression «word of the kingdom». When God speaks to us, He teaches us higher spiritual realities. His words are Spirit and life and are a seed that can sprout, grow and bear fruit in our hearts. Every revelation we receive through the Holy Spirit holds this potential, and the enemy of our souls knows this very well. Therefore, if he cannot prevent the seed from falling into your heart, he will try to steal it from you so that it cannot grow there.

Have you ever heard a sermon and been overwhelmed by the message, only to completely forget it a few days later? If you don't learn to treasure God's words, to meditate on them, to examine them, and to hold them in your heart, your life will be as barren and void of life.

When the Lord speaks to you, the thoughts you receive are not the fruit of your understanding, so you cannot find them through reasoning. They are a revelation, like a download. By way of comparison, if you receive an e-mail message with an attachment and you delete it, the only way to find it is to receive it again.

We must understand that meditation allows God's revelation to take root in us until it becomes our new reality, our paradigm. While the seed of God's word carries within itself the supernatural life of the kingdom, you must be aware that the enemy will equally supernaturally oppose its taking root in you. It is therefore necessary to be proactive to retain and preserve what God tells you or shows you.

You will need to meditate on what God is telling you so that your thoughts can be changed.

It is normal that it takes time and reflection to digest, absorb and assimilate the revelations that the Lord gives us. This process cannot be done without meditation, which is a way of reflecting, weighing, contemplating, considering what God has said.

When God reveals a truth to us, it comes to confront the lie within us. We then need to meditate on it, that is to say, to repeat in us what we have received so that it is imprinted in our hearts.

Now the angel of the LORD came and sat under the terebinth at Ophrah, which belonged to Joash the Abiezrite, while his son Gideon was beating out wheat in the winepress to hide it from the Midianites. And the angel of the LORD appeared to him and said to him, "The LORD is with you, O mighty man of valor." And Gideon said to him, "Please, my Lord, if the LORD is with us, why then has all this happened to us? And where are all his wonderful deeds that our fathers recounted to us, saying, 'Did not the LORD bring us up from Egypt?' But now the LORD has forsaken us and given us into the hand of Midian." And the LORD turned to him and said, "Go in this might of yours and save Israel from the hand of Midian; do not I send you?" And he said to him, "Please, Lord, how can I save Israel? Behold, my clan is the weakest in Manasseh, and I am the least in my father's house." And the LORD said to him, "But I will be with you, and you shall strike the Midianites as one man."

(Judges 6.11-16)

Gideon received words from God that brought him into his destiny. What the Lord declared to him («valiant hero») confronted what he thought of himself; the word of God redefined his identity. After talking with the angel, after testing the revelation with the fleeces, Gideon acted like a hero. The word of God that he received, tested (examined, tried) and believed produced courage in him and changed him profoundly (I recommend that you reread his entire story in Judges 6 and imagine yourself in his place). Notice that God agreed to confirm His word several times so that Gideon could obey it by faith. You must know that it is normal and desirable to seek confirmations when we listen to God. The more important the subject, the greater the risk of error, and the more different confirmations should be sought. For his part, Gideon asked for three confirmations and was then encouraged by the dream of an enemy soldier interpreted by his comrade in arms.

It is interesting to note that the confirmations that God gave to Gideon were of a different nature. The first was an angelic apparition accompanied by a word. The second was fire coming out of the stone to consume the offering. The third came when the angel ascended into the smoke of the sacrifice. The next two were tangible physical signs (the fleece), and finally we can retain the dream made by an enemy with interpretation. Let us emphasize that it is good not to rely solely on what one receives personally when seeking confirmations. Here are some ways to find out:

- ·Read the Bible consistently and let God speak to you as you read.
- ·Ask someone to pray for you without telling them what is on your mind.

- ·Note if what happens around you, is going in the same direction as what you have received.
- ·Sleep to dream.
- ·Please be patient, you may not get all the confirmations on the same day. Move forward by faith as they come to you.

After receiving the requested confirmations, Gideon obeyed by faith and accomplished increasingly daring feats. He put his life in danger when knocking down the altar of Baal because the villagers wanted to kill him. Then he took risks by going to fight a huge army with only 300 soldiers. Some people sometimes mock Gideon for asking for confirmation with the fleeces, but let us note that he was not an indecisive man: once he knew for sure that God was speaking to him, he obeyed him to the letter and showed courage. Following a divine exhortation, he even went to the enemy camp with his servant to listen to the conversation of two soldiers. How could this man who called himself the smallest in Israel, who thought that God had forsaken him, act with such recklessness and face more and more enemies? Unquestionably, God's words about his identity and destiny transformed him. Likewise, the more you listen to God and drink from his source, the more you will see yourself as he sees you and the more you will act as he expects of you. Expect to experience great inner change!

Preciously keep God's words as love letters.

When I was engaged to Sylvie, we lived a few weeks of geographical separation for the service of God. She was in Romania and I was in France. So we wrote to each other, and although we have been married for 17 years , and we have moved 5 times so far, we still have these love letters. We keep them with care. In the same way, your prayer journal is your story with God, it is the love letter that He sends to you, so keep it carefully.

Tips for keeping a journal

Before ending this chapter, I would like to give you some tips for keeping a journal. First of all, use a journal that you can keep and enjoy writing in.

Avoid loose leaves that are easy to misplace. Begin by putting in the current date and then reread what God has previously communicated to you. Go back more or less according to the time you have available.

Write down the questions, prayers, and thanks you give to God, clearly distinguishing them from what you receive in prayer.

If you take notes on a phone, tablet or computer, you can easily search your diary, which is very handy; it also allows you to copy and paste.

Personally, I use a style sheet in Word with different colors for each heading: dreams, prophecies, what I receive from God, visions and testimonies. I also use headings for days and months to make it easier to navigate through my journal.

I advise you to regularly take time to reread your monthly or yearly journal. At the end of the year, summarize the promises, revelations, and visions you have received from God and their accomplishments.

I am personally very encouraged when I reread my journal. I see my progress, God's faithfulness, and it keeps me focused on what the Lord has told me. Remember, the most important thing is to have a regular conversation with God. I invite you to pray with me now:

Lord, I ask your forgiveness for all the words that I let fall to the ground out of ignorance or disbelief. I choose to feed on every word that comes out of your mouth. I choose to cherish each one as a treasure. Speak, your servant listens. Holy Spirit, teach me to meditate on Your words so that I may be transformed and fulfill my destiny. Father, please give me now the encouragement I will need in the coming fights. I beg you to keep the thief out of my life so that your word may germinate and bear fruit in me. In the name of Jesus, Amen.

I will pray for you now. Read the following prayer and then take a few minutes of silence before God to let Him work in you.

Father, I pray for your child that he/she will become a faithful steward of your words, that he/she will treat them with respect and honor, that his/her faith will grow to believe you. I pray that you will sharpen his or her ability to examine what comes from you and discern what is good. That he/she may be protected in this way from false paths and from those who would lead him/her astray. May your strength be imparted to him/her as he/she is nourished by your words, that he/she may be changed to think like you and walk according to his/her identity within you. May your reign come into his or her life.In the name of Jesus, Amen.

Practical exercise

Now it's time to put into practice what you've just read! Relax physically and mentally and take your journal.

Play instrumental music, e.g. by clicking on the following address:

entdi.eu/piano

Before moving on to the next chapter, take a moment to be intimate with God, reread your journal, and listen to Him.

I suggest that you ask God about a topic with a prayer partner and then compare what you receive.

Ask a friend to read what you have received from God in recent times. It will inspire them and make them thirsty to listen to God.

THE SHEPHERD'S FRIEND

CHAPTER 9

DEEPENING THE DIALOGUE

I find that some people, after hearing God speak to them, do not seek to know more. This is not a lack of interest, but rather lies that block them in their fellowship with God. What the Lord began to tell you was not a unique privilege, but the beginning of a deepening of your relationship.

Sometimes you may be afraid to disturb someone when talking to them, especially if they are a stranger and do not look inviting. On the other hand, if we recognize a friend, that he or she is smiling, and our eyes meet, we will be more easily inclined to start a conversation.

It is the same with God. When we are sure that He wants to talk to us, it becomes more natural to have a conversation. Here is what I received in prayer while preparing this chapter.

I long to commune with you. It is this communion, this friendship that I seek. Do not be afraid of me. I am here for each one of you, you have my full attention. Come closer to learn more. As a little child asks questions to his/her parents, don't be embarrassed. You won't always get the answer you want, but I will guide you with love.

God longs to commune with you

It is this communion, this friendship that he seeks.

Behold, I stand at the door and knock. If anyone hears my voice and opens the door, I will come in to him and eat with him, and he with me.

(Revelation 3:20)

God wants to be in communion with us. Jesus said he will come to supper with the one who loves Him. In a supper with friends, we discuss, we engage on different levels, we go from light to serious, from sad to joyful subjects. This is the kind of relationship that the Lord wants with us.

Jesus made this promise to us, and like all God's promises, we must grasp it by faith. This means that we must believe that Jesus really wants to spend time with us. Being in communion with us is God's idea, it is His will, it is His desire.

When we are in communion, in a relationship of friendship with God, he speaks to us about the things of our heart, about him, about those around us, he also gives us advice or warnings to protect us.

In a friendly relationship, we also exchange words of encouragement and affection. These words are not meant to communicate information, but to comfort. When we feel loved and appreciated, our self-esteem grows and we feel more self-confident.

The Lord wants to build your identity in you during these times of intimacy. So don't be surprised that He often speaks to you with comforting and encouraging words. Jesus said that it is from the abundance of the heart that the mouth speaks. God is love, he is benevolent. It is therefore normal that his words reflect his nature.

In a friendly relationship, we also congratulate each other and rejoice in successes, we comfort each other when we are sad. Don't think that the Lord has no time to waste with your emotions. Don't think that He is too busy or that your problems don't deserve His attention.

Finally, in a friendship, one appreciates the fact of being together as much as the content of the exchanges. Sometimes we even stay together without talking. In the same way, God appreciates your company, even in silence. I encourage you to say to him now: «Father, I come to you to give you a hug, receive my affection and my love. «Then be quiet and stay close to him for a few minutes in silence.

Maintaining this intimate relationship will facilitate your approach to God in times of trouble, questioning or difficult circumstances. You will learn to recognize the manifestation of His affection and you will not be disappointed if you do not get answers to your questions. This is what David was experiencing when he wrote Psalm 131.

O LORD, my heart is not lifted up; my eyes are not raised too high; I do not occupy myself with things too great and too marve-

lous for me. But I have calmed and quieted my soul, like a weaned child with its mother; like a weaned child is my soul within me.

(Psalm 131:1-2)

If the Lord does not answer you, let His affection and comfort calm your soul. In a conversation, we ask each other questions. We see in the Bible that God dialogues with his children and does not say everything at once. For example, we see that God draws the attention of the prophet Jeremiah by saying, «What do you see? »

And the word of the LORD came to me, saying, "Jeremiah, what do you see?" And I said, "I see an almond branch." Then the LORD said to me, "You have seen well, for I am watching over my word to perform it."

(Jeremiah 1.11-12)

Once Jeremiah enters the dialogue, he receives a message from God. Chances are that you are receiving visions from God without understanding what they mean, because God wants you to ask him. I regularly ask God questions, but sometimes I also feel that he wants me to ask him a certain question. These moments are often profound revelations. So open yourself to the idea that God is asking you questions. God sometimes wants to talk about a particular subject and he is waiting for certain questions to be asked. One day I had the thought of asking him how he was doing. He told me about his sadness about the lost who suffer far from him.

Another day we were discussing our friendship and he told me that friends often think about each other. So I asked him what he was thinking about (Sylvie often asks me this question, especially when I'm not thinking about anything).

The Lord replied that he was thinking of me and that he was proud of my progress, which astounded and encouraged me.

And the LORD called Samuel again the third time. And he arose and went to Eli and said, "Here I am, for you called me." Then Eli perceived that the LORD was calling the boy.

(1 Samuel 3.8)

Samuel was challenged by God, but he did not answer him, he did not engage in conversation and therefore received nothing more. Eli then taught the young boy to recognize God («Speak Lord») and to dialogue with him («Your servant is listening»). If we don't understand that the Lord likes to talk to us, we will just hear our first name and miss what he wanted to tell us.

Do not be afraid of God

God is there for each one of us, you have his full attention. There are many dialogues with God in the Bible. From Adam in Genesis to the apostle John in Revelation, human beings have dialogued with their Creator. What interests us here is to develop a relationship of friendship with him. Let us consider the one who was called God's friend, Abraham, the father of believers.

and the Scripture was fulfilled that says, "Abraham believed God, and it was counted to him as righteousness"—and he was called a friend of God.

(James 2.23)

We saw earlier that Jesus promised to come to supper with the one who loves him. Abraham had this experience in

Genesis chapter 18. In fact, God came to Abraham's house for supper without being invited. He knew that Abraham would invite him, so he came to his house accompanied by two angels. He then spoke with him and Sarah about their future son, the subject of the promise. As Abraham walked him hom God wanted to discuss a sensitive subject with him.

> *he LORD said, "Shall I hide from Abraham what I am about to do.*
>
> *(Genesis 18.17)*

As we saw in chapter seven, God reveals his secrets to his friends. So God took the initiative to warn Abraham about the impending destruction of Sodom, the city in which his nephew Lot resided. It was following this revelation that a famous dialogue of intercession began.

Then Abraham drew near and said, "Will you indeed sweep away the righteous with the wicked? Suppose there are fifty righteous within the city. Will you then sweep away the place and not spare it for the fifty righteous who are in it? Far be it from you to do such a thing, to put the righteous to death with the wicked, so that the righteous fare as the wicked! Far be that from you! Shall not the Judge of all the earth do what is just?" And the LORD said, "If I find at Sodom fifty righteous in the city, I will spare the whole place for their sake."

> *Abraham answered and said, "Behold, I have undertaken to speak to the Lord, I who am but dust and ashes. Suppose five of the fifty righteous are lacking. Will you destroy the whole city for lack of five?" And he said, "I will not destroy it if I find forty-five there." Again he spoke to him and said, "Suppose forty are found there." He answered, "For the sake of forty I will not do it." Then he said,*

"Oh let not the Lord be angry, and I will speak. Suppose thirty are found there." He answered, "I will not do it, if I find thirty there." He said, "Behold, I have undertaken to speak to the Lord. Suppose twenty are found there." He answered, "For the sake of twenty I will not destroy it." Then he said, "Oh let not the Lord be angry, and I will speak again but this once. Suppose ten are found there." He answered, "For the sake of ten I will not destroy it." And the LORD went his way, when he had finished speaking to Abraham, and Abraham returned to his place.

(Genesis 18:23-33)

If Abraham had had a different relationship with God, he would have simply said, «Let it be done according to your will! «But the Lord knew that Abraham was his friend and he knew his heart. So Abraham called upon God's compassion and justice to spare the righteous innocent. He began with mentioning the possible presence of fifty righteous people in the city. God granted him what he asked for. Then Abraham, knowing the sins of Sodom, realized that it might be difficult to find fifty righteous people. So he gradually decreased the number to ten and then stopped. Abraham was seized by the fear of God, and what seemed to him to be of great boldness did not seem to have bothered God. Notice that it was Abraham who apologized for interceding, but God did not express any form of resistance or irritation. Clearly, Abraham stops negotiating because he is afraid that God will be angry with him if he continues.

God wanted to have this conversation

God made the appointment, he addressed the subject and continued the conversation as long as Abraham wanted to discuss it. I believe that without the friendship between Abraham and God, this dialogue would not have taken place. Imagine with me what would have happened if Abraham had not dared to say anything to God. Conversely, what would have happened in Sodom if Abraham had continued to talk with God?

The end of this conversation seems to show that Abraham had more compassion than God and that God's limit was ten righteous to spare the city, but the rest of the text shows the opposite. Here is the last exchange between Lot and the angels who took him out of Sodom:

> *Behold, your servant has found favor in your sight, and you have shown me great kindness in saving my life. But I cannot escape to the hills, lest the disaster overtake me and I die. Behold, this city is near enough to flee to, and it is a little one. Let me escape there—is it not a little one?—and my life will be saved!" He said to him, "Behold, I grant you this favor also, that I will not overthrow the city of which you have spoken.*
>
> (Genesis 19.19-21)

The angels took Lot out of the city with his wife and two daughters (four people). His wife was turned into a statue of salt. The city of Zoar, which was also to be destroyed, was spared, not because of ten righteous people as Abraham had dared to ask, but because of three people. When we add the fact that the daughters of Lot committed incest and that the apostle Peter calls Lot a righteous man, we realize that the city of Zoar was spared for only one righteous man: Lot. We thus conclude that God's goodness and mercy are always greater than what we can believe.

With this explanation, I hope you understand that your perception of God can greatly influence your dialogue with Him. Don't let fear prevent you from communicating with your Heavenly Father.

There is no fear in love, but perfect love casts out fear. For fear has to do with punishment, and whoever fears has not been perfected in love.

(1 John 4.18)

Remember that the Lord loves you and His purpose is not to punish you, for Jesus suffered the punishment that gives you peace with God. His desire is to be in communion with you. If you believe Him by faith, you will be free to approach Him without fear.

Ask questions. The worst thing that can happen is that God doesn't answer you what you want to hear!

No longer do I call you servants, for the servant does not know what his master is doing; but I have called you friends, for all that I have heard from my Father I have made known to you.

(John 15:15)

Jesus made it clear to his disciples that he lets his friends know what we need. It is God's intention to reveal his will to you, and he wants to reveal more than you think. Because the Lord wants to be your friend, he does not just transfer information to you, but seeks dialogue. Will you collaborate with him? Will you take the time to have dinner with him so that he can reveal his secrets to you over coffee?

I have a friend who is truly a man of God with a prophetic ability in his life. After his conversion, during his adolescence, he wanted to become friends with God. Every day when he came home from school, he had tea with the Lord. He would tell him about his day while sipping his cup. He would stay with him until he had drunk all his tea, but since the water was boiling, it took a long time. My friend is now receiving very specific revelations because he has been able to cultivate this intimate relationship with God. Indeed, there are no shortcuts.

The closer we are to the Lord, the more he shares with us the secrets of his heart. In everyday life, adding a friend on Facebook has nothing to do with a friendship that develops between two people who regularly spend time together. It is the same with God.

Get closer to learn more

As a small child asks questions to his parents, don't be embarrassed. Don't think that if God speaks, the meaning will always be obvious right away. In fact, the Lord likes to talk and spend time with us. So he likes to spike our curiosity, and also to see us walking by faith. Personally, when I announce good news, I like to think about how I am going to share it in order to arouse the curiosity of the receiver. This way, he is waiting for something and is excited before he even knows what I am going to tell him. It is a real pleasure to see my daughters' eyes sparkling when they are waiting for news, their mouths open, ready to drink my words. I believe that God feels the same pleasure with us: He likes our attention to be fully focused on Him. He doesn't want to miss any of the joy we will experience when we hear his words.

What excites God is our faith. It means that He takes pleasure in it. If you want to please the Lord, dare to believe that He wants to talk to you, dare to examine what you receive from Him, even if the impression is very subtle. When I play hide-and-seek with my daughters, I sometimes give them clues by calling their first name or banging on a wall to get their attention. The joy they feel when they follow this hint is also mine. So instead of saying, «It can't be God because I don't understand! «Instead, try saying, «What if it were God? Lord, is it you? What does that mean? »

The prophet Zechariah received visions and had to ask the meaning of them to the angel who accompanied him.

And the angel who talked with me came again and woke me, like a man who is awakened out of his sleep. And he said to me, "What do you see?" I said, "I see, and behold, a lampstand all of gold, with a bowl on the top of it, and seven lamps on it, with seven lips on each of the lamps that are on the top of it. And there are two olive trees by it, one on the right of the bowl and the other on its left." And I said to the angel who talked with me, "What are these, my lord?" Then the angel who talked with me answered and said to me, "Do you not know what these are?" I said, "No, my lord." Then he said to me, "This is the word of the LORD to Zerubbabel: Not by might, nor by power, but by my Spirit, says the LORD of hosts. Who are you, O great mountain? Before Zerubbabel you shall become a plain. And he shall bring forward the top stone amid shouts of 'Grace, grace to it!'"

Then the word of the LORD came to me, saying, "The hands of Zerubbabel have laid the foundation of this house; his hands shall also complete it. Then you will know that the LORD of hosts has sent me to you. For whoever has despised the day of small things shall rejoice, and shall see the plumb line in the hand of Zerubbabel.

> *"These seven are the eyes of the LORD, which range through the whole earth." Then I said to him, "What are these two olive trees on the right and the left of the lampstand?" And a second time I answered and said to him, "What are these two branches of the olive trees, which are beside the two golden pipes from which the golden oil is poured out?" He said to me, "Do you not know what these are?" I said, "No, my lord." Then he said, "These are the two anointed ones who stand by the Lord of the whole earth."*
>
> *(Zechariah 4.1-14)*

Zechariah is awakened by an angel to see what God wants to show him, but the vision is mysterious and symbolic. The prophet does not understand it, so he asks the angel about it, but the angel does not answer him. Zechariah insists and asks the question a second time. The angel is then surprised at the prophet's ignorance and then communicates to him the general meaning of the vision and a message about Zerubbabel. Don't you think that we, too, would have needed the interpretation ? If Zechariah, while accompanied by an angel, had to insist on having the meaning of the vision, we too can persevere to receive from God the interpretation of what we have received. Remember: why would God show you something incomprehensible? There would be no point. The good news is that we can expect to receive and understand the meaning of what God shows us.

When you read the Bible, look at how God interacts with men and women, put yourself in their shoes, and learn from them about what you can experience for yourself. You can ask God questions like :

- ·What else do you want to tell me, Lord?
- ·I don't understand, what do you mean by that?
- ·Lord, is it you who is speaking to me?
- ·Lord, why are you showing me this image?
- ·Lord what does this mean?
- ·Can you give me a biblical basis for this?
- ·Why is this important?

You may not always get the answer you want, but God will guide you with love.

God is at the same time close as a friend, but he is also the master of the universe, the Creator, the Almighty. You cannot interrogate him in order to force him to speak. If you remember that the Lord only says what He wants to say when you ask Him questions, you can rest in peace if He does not answer you. Imagine that you ask a friend a question he doesn't want to answer and he simply changes the subject. If you have a minimum of interpersonal knowledge, you will conclude that he didn't want to discuss it and that he has his reasons. You will respect him and allow him to confide in you when he feels it is appropriate.

It would be ridiculous in this kind of situation to decide not to talk to your friend anymore. Yet this is often what we do with God. You ask him a question and don't get an answer, or the Lord decides to talk about something else and you conclude that it's not worth talking to him and you never speak to him again.

There are no effective methods or means of pressure to make God speak. Become his friend, listen to what He has to say to you, don't let his words fall to the ground and he will come and reveal his secrets to you. Remember that the Lord is not irritated by your questions, but do not be offended by his answers. Sometimes I ask Him about certain matters and receive an unrelated answer. It is as if he were saying to me, «I have something more important to communicate to you today. «It's a bit like a friend changing conversations because he has news to share. This is what happened to the disciples before Jesus ascended to heaven:

> *So when they had come together, they asked him, "Lord, will you at this time restore the kingdom to Israel?" He said to them, "It is not for you to know times or seasons that the Father has fixed by his own authority. But you will receive power when the Holy Spirit has come upon you, and you will be my witnesses in Jerusalem and in all Judea and Samaria, and to the end of the earth."*
>
> *(Acts of the Apostles 1.6-8)*

If you maintain the goal of developing your relationship and friendship with the Holy Spirit, you will protect yourself from the pitfalls that those who think they have THE method to make God speak will encounter. To take a typical example, the subject of Jesus' return has been the subject of many prophecies. Several authors have written books with specific dates. Yet, we must agree that Jesus said that he was coming back soon, that we would be surprised and that it was important to be prepared. When you listen to God, you focus on what is really important. For example, in the case of the disciples, Pentecost was far more foundational than the date of Israel's restoration. So let God change your priorities. What's important is what He says is important, not what you think is important. For example, there have been times when I have wanted revelations about this or that subject when God wanted to talk to me about my relationship with my wife. Likewise, you might want to get indications about the end of an ordeal and the Lord might simply encourage you to persevere, you might want keys to an interpersonal situation and He might actually ask you to change your attitude or repent. Yes, you are God's friend, but don't forget that your friend is God!

I invite you to make this statement with me:

I am a child of God, my Heavenly Father loves me and thinks of me. Jesus calls me His friend and He wants to have dinner with me. I am invited to commune with the Holy Spirit. I am free to come to him through Jesus, I do not disturb him, for he wants to be with me. I give up the fear that God will get angry if I ask him questions. I reject the lie that I need to understand right away what God is revealing to me if I am spiritual. I accept that I don't have all the answers to my questions, I renounce the lie that I can force God to answer me. I come to you, Father, like a child full of questions and I let you guide me with your love. Father, here I am, to listen to you and to dialogue with you.

I will pray for you now. Read the following prayer and then take a few minutes of silence before God to let Him work in you.

Father, thank you for the reality of communion with you. I pray for your son/daughter so that he/she may experience all the richness in union with Jesus Christ. I pray for a deepening, an even greater thirst, a childlike faith that explores your kingdom without fear. I bring you all the emotional limitations, defensive walls, parental projections and false images of God that could limit this fellowship. Holy Spirit, come and reveal them and replace them with the truth of Your love. May Your child be added to the number of Your friends, in the name of Jesus, Amen.

Practical exercise

Now it's time to put into practice what you've just read! Relax physically and mentally and take your journal.

Play instrumental music, for example typing the following address :

entdi.eu/piano

Take your journal and discuss with God, I suggest you ask Him what He wants to talk to you about. Ask him what questions he wants you to ask him.

You can also ask him to identify the fears or blockages that limit your communion with him.

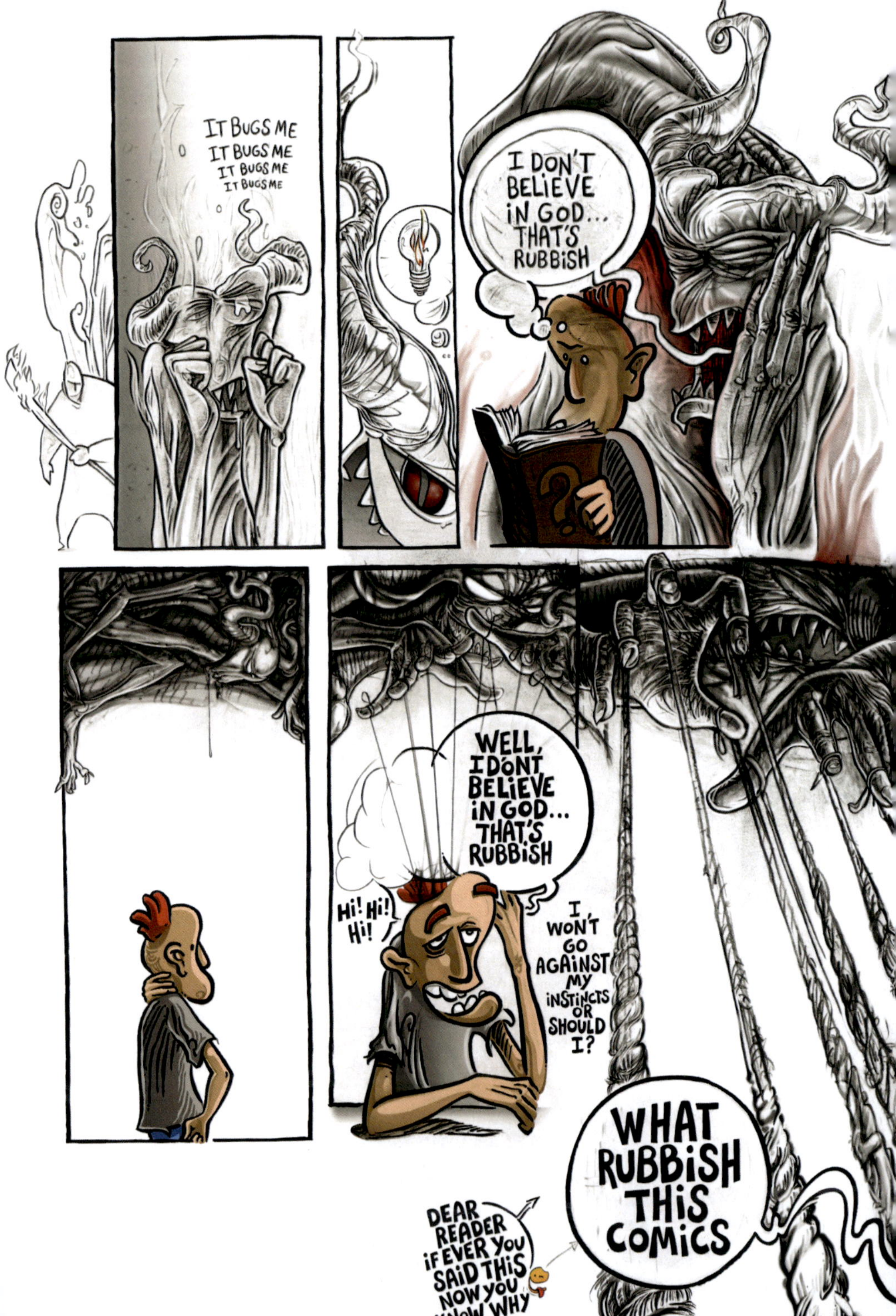
IT BUGS ME
IT BUGS ME
IT BUGS ME
IT BUGS ME
I DON'T BELIEVE IN GOD... THAT'S RUBBISH
WELL, I DON'T BELIEVE IN GOD... THAT'S RUBBISH
HI! HI! HI!
I WON'T GO AGAINST MY INSTINCTS OR SHOULD I?
WHAT RUBBISH THIS COMICS
DEAR READER IF EVER YOU SAID THIS NOW YOU KNOW WHY

CHAPTER 10.

DISCOVERING THE TRUTH

Jesus came so that we can be completely free. Freedom manifests itself in the possibility of acting without hindrance according to our will. Yet we often find ourselves unable to act or think according to the Gospel. We may even experience a sense of captivity, without being able to define it. As you listen to the Holy Spirit, you will discover what holds you captive and how to be set free from it. This is what I received in preparing this chapter:

> *I have come so that you may be free, completely free. Free from what you are not aware of, but which holds you captive. I am the liberator. The more you listen to me, the less power and influence the enemy will have in your life. Renounce lies and embrace the truths I reveal to you through my Spirit. I want to lead you to peaceful waters and green pastures.*

Jesus came so that you may be free, completely free.

So Jesus said to the Jews who had believed him, "If you abide in my word, you are truly my disciples, and you will know the truth, and the truth will set you free." They answered him, "We are offspring of Abraham and have never been enslaved to anyone. How is it that you say, 'You will become free'?" Jesus answered them, "Truly, truly, I say to you, everyone who practices sin is a slave to sin. The slave does not remain in the house forever; the son remains forever. So if the Son sets you free, you will be free indeed.

(John 8.31-36)

This famous text is often used for evangelism. It explains to people that when discovering Jesus, the Truth, they will be free. Yet the text is clear, Jesus is speaking to the Jews who had believed in him, that is to say to the disciples. He affirms that the discovery of the Truth and its understanding makes them free. He does not say to them: «You have discovered the truth and it has set you free. «He uses a future, which implies that his listeners are not yet entirely free. That is why the disciples react so strongly. They do not understand why Jesus speaks to them about freedom when they are free men (unlike the slaves who were very numerous in the society of that time) and they already believe in Him. Their reaction shows that it is possible to be captive without realizing it. We all experience this form of captivity at different levels. Jesus said, «You will know the truth. When we do not know the truth, we probably believe a lie. But we are captive to the lies we believe. It is perfectly possible to believe lies while believing in Jesus. In reality, everyone believes lies. If we didn't believe any lies, we would be walking on water!

We learned these lies from other people. For example, when someone told you after an accident or injury: «God is punishing you! «You may have believed the lie that God is cruel.

You have accepted other lies after certain experiences in your life. For example, if you have been repeatedly betrayed or abandoned by loved ones, you may have believed the lie that you cannot trust anyone. This makes it hard for you to even trust a friend. This blockage is a lack of freedom that stems from the lie you believed and still believe.

Other lies have been sown in you through repetition. If, for example, your parents or teachers have often told you, «You're a good-for-nothing,» chances are you've come to believe it. You may not have this thought in your mind all the time, but it can act as a filter to keep you from trying and succeeding. You may become paralyzed, captive.

These lies are for us truths, we don't think about them. They define our paradigm, or to put it simply, it's like having colored glasses in front of our eyes and no longer realizing it. The good news is that Jesus Christ is the liberator. Real freedom comes when you can do something that wasn't possible before. Discovering the truth will therefore allow you to experience new things.

As we saw in Chapter Two, the enemy also wants to talk to you, and if you believe a lie, it gives him a point of access to your heart to manipulate you. It is therefore essential, if you want to live out God's plans for happiness, to seek total freedom in Jesus. For example, if I believe the lie that forgiveness is an act of weakness, I will not easily forgive and so I deprive myself of the benefits of forgiveness and allow the enemy to torment me through my bitterness. Often we are not aware of these lies. But when we find that we cannot forgive, we feel unable to do it, we are like a captive, but we do not discern the chains enemy has us wrapped in.

God wants to free you from the lies you unconsciously believe.

And I will ask the Father, and he will give you another Helper, to be with you forever, even the Spirit of truth, whom the world cannot receive, because it neither sees him nor knows him. You know him, for he dwells with you and will be in you.

(John 14:16-17)

All these lies are stored in us, in our subconscious. We therefore do not have access to them through reasoning, which is why the psychological exercises of introspection have limited effectiveness. It is obvious that it is impossible to solve a problem as long as we are unaware of its existence. The Holy Spirit was present when you first believed this lie, because He is God and knows all about you. Because He dwells in you, He has access to the depths of your soul. Moreover, he is the Spirit of truth and he reveals the lie. He is therefore your best ally in uncovering the lies that hold you captive and being set free from them. Certainly, the Holy Spirit has the power to bring to light what is hidden in the darkness.

The power of the lie comes from the fact that we adhere to it and deliberately submit to it until we know the truth. We are voluntarily, though unconsciously, attached to the lie.

The Spirit of truth lives within us, but we must intentionally renounce the lie, detach ourselves from it, and cling to the truth in order to regain freedom.

Jesus is the liberator

The more you listen to God, the less power and influence the enemy will have in your life.

> *But he who enters by the door is the shepherd of the sheep. To him the gatekeeper opens. The sheep hear his voice, and he calls his own sheep by name and leads them out. When he has brought out all his own, he goes before them, and the sheep follow him, for they know his voice. A stranger they will not follow, but they will flee from him, for they do not know the voice of strangers.*
>
> *(John 10.2-5)*

We explored this text in Chapter Two. Satan is the father of lies, he is the author of lies. When you believe a lie, you follow the enemy instead of following the good shepherd. The devil does not use force to lead us into paths of destruction. It is enough for him to make us believe lies so that we voluntarily and unconsciously walk towards death. To renounce lies is to refuse to follow the enemy, to flee from him and to be led by the good shepherd. To renounce lies is to change direction, path, destiny. To renounce lies is to enter into the plans of happiness and peace that God has prepared for you.

Renounce lies and accept the truths that God reveals to you by His Spirit.

Some of our difficulties have their origin in the sin of those around us. But much of the fulfillment of the enemy's plans to destroy us in our lives comes from the fact that we voluntarily follow him without realizing it. So it is important to ask God whether we are following him or whether we are following the enemy without being aware of it.

Jesus is the truth, but this general truth is not enough to make us truly free. We must have the truth equivalent to every lie we believe. It is God's will that you be free. So you can simply ask the Lord to reveal to you the lies you believe in a particular area, for example, about Him, about yourself, or about those around you. You can do it very simply this way:

Father, what lie do I believe about such a subject?

Once the lie is identified, you can ask the Lord what is the precise truth you should believe. Remember that when the Holy Spirit speaks, His words are creative, they produce life. The truth He will therefore communicate to you will not just be information, but a revelation, a divine downloading into the depths of your heart. It is the power of the word that comes out of the mouth of God. If a lie that has been sown in your heart has been able to produce a tree and fruit for years, how much more a truth sown by the Holy Spirit in your heart will grow and bear fruit for this life and eternity! Simply renouncing the lie and confessing the truth will trigger a paradigm shift. You will then be able to gradually walk in this new freedom.

Most of the time, a person is behind a lie that we believed. It is therefore necessary that you forgive that person, even if they were not aware of the effect of their words or actions on you.

God can reveal to you the lie you believe in the form of a thought, a vision, a dream or a memory. If you ask him the question I have suggested, he will answer you. It is also possible that he will draw your attention to a lie you believe without you having asked him the question first. So be attentive, discovering each lie and renouncing it will allow you to live more freely.

When the Holy Spirit reveals a truth to us, we can experience many forms of resistance. The first comes from the fact that we do not like change. Changing the paradigm requires the humility to accept that I was wrong. Remember that the Bible is the standard for truth. If, therefore, the Holy Spirit reveals to you a biblical truth that you have so far neglected, ignored or underestimated, decide to submit your mind to the Word of God. Regularly confessing this specific truth with faith will allow the Holy Spirit to renew your mind. You will be truly free when you spontaneously act according to the truth and no longer according to a lie. This process can take time, so it is necessary to write down what God will reveal to you so that you can meditate on it regularly.

The second resistance is related to faith. It is possible that you may intellectually believe the truth without attaching your heart to it. So you may think you are following God while your heart follows the enemy. Let's take an example. Most Christians know that Jesus said, «Don't worry about anything. «Yet many of God's children worry about running out of money. This worry shows that their hearts believe that God cannot provide for their needs. If therefore the Holy Spirit reveals to you that you believe a lie when your mind claims otherwise, do not reject what the Holy Spirit has shown you. To align your heart with the truth, you must decide to believe this truth by faith and hold on to it. I would like to illustrate this in the following way: you can hear Jesus calling you by name and recognize His voice on an intellectual level. Only when you decide to follow the sound of his voice and get physically moving will you demonstrate your faith.

To use the example of forgiveness, Jesus can tell you that it is courageous to forgive, and that it is a proof of spiritual maturity (which is true and biblical). You will need to decide to forgive based on this truth. You will be truly free when you see forgiveness as God sees it.

As a pastor, I often have to pray for and counsel people. If I talk to their intelligence, the result is limited. I have found that it is far more effective to guide the person to receive truths from the Holy Spirit. The effect in the heart surpasses all my arguments. You, too, can guide someone in prayer in this way: «Let us ask the Holy Spirit to speak to you. Repeat after me, 'Holy Spirit, what is the lie I believe about this? Wait a few moments and then ask the person what has gone up inside them. Then have them repeat, «Holy Spirit, what is the truth you want me to believe? «Wait again and then ask the person what spontaneously came into his or her heart. Consider whether it is biblical, and then help them to renounce the lie and confess the truth. Chances are that this will be accompanied by an emotional response because God will show his love.

God wants to lead you to the still waters and green pastures.

The good shepherd leads his sheep at the sound of his voice, he does not keep them on a leash to force them to follow him. That is why the lies that hold your heart prevent you from following Jesus in the green pastures. If you become free from lies and walk in the truth, you will be able to follow the Lord and experience what He has promised you, instead of just hoping for it. So you will experience more peace. Your soul will be filled, satiated and refreshed. Discovering the truth will allow your heart to follow what you wanted to do with your head. It is a process: the more you cling to it, the more you will be amazed at how many lies you believed. So you will experience a growing and progressive fulfillment.

God is also the God of restitution. As you grasp the truth, you will become aware of what the enemy has deprived you of and what has been stolen from you.

Do not then give in to anger and bitterness, but pray that God will grant you double restitution, as He did for Job.

And the LORD restored the fortunes of Job, when he had prayed for his friends. And the LORD gave Job twice as much as he had before.

(Job 42:10)

As you regain your freedom, your field of influence will increase, because the people around you will see that you are experiencing a freedom greater than theirs. Do not keep the treasures of truth that Jesus revealed to you for yourself. Get revenge for your suffering by freeing other captives through the truth of Jesus. The enemy uses the same lies with everyone. Many people around you are therefore captives to the same lies as you are. By simply sharing the truth you have discovered, you can change the lives of those around you, communicating hope, faith and life to them. Don't let shame muzzle you. Instead, become a public denouncer of the enemy's strategies and deceptions, become an ambassador for Christ the liberator.

Lies are hidden deep in hearts. As it was the case with you, others are unaware of their captivity. Simply share your testimony, even if it doesn't seem appropriate at first glance. You will be amazed at the number of people who will be touched by what you have experienced and who in turn will share their stories with you. So don't underestimate the impact of your testimony.

I suggest you pray with me:

Thank you Jesus because you came so that I would be completely free. I refuse today to be satisfied with virtual or promised freedom. Thank you Father because you have put your Spirit in me, the Spirit of truth. Holy Spirit, please open my eyes and ears to the lies I believe. Holy Spirit, I open my heart to you to uproot the lies that have been sown from my birth to this day. Please reveal to me the truth that will set me free. Lord Jesus, thank you for setting me free so that I may enter the green pastures you have for me. Lead me to the sound of your voice. Father, I beg you to restore to me all that has been stolen from me in my relationship with you, in my relationship with others. May my heart and my thoughts be in accord with your Word. In the name of Jesus, Amen.

I will pray for you now. Read the following prayer and then take a few minutes of silence before God to let Him work in you.

Thank you Father, because your promises of freedom are real. In the name of Jesus, may your light shine on your child, may the lies be revealed. I pray that you grant him/her a spirit of revelation that makes him/her know the truth.

I pray for convictions, inspired thoughts, dreams, and visions. Thank you Fulher for opening the spiritual eyes and ears of your child. May false concepts, demon doctrines, and lies be brought to light and destroyed by Your truth, in the name of Jesus.

I declare freedom. More freedom in his relationship with you, more freedom in his heart, more freedom to obey you, more freedom to love the people around him/her.

I declare that the enemy may speak, but that your child will run away from him/her, he/she will stop following him/her, because he/she will recognize the lie and walk at the sound of your voice.

Thank you because you will lead your child to the green pastures. I pray that your peace will increase in his life and that his testimony will set the captives free, in the name of Jesus, Amen.

Practice exercise

Now it's time to put into practice what you've just read! Relax physically and mentally and take your journal.

Play instrumental music, for example by clicking on the following address:

entdi.eu/piano

Focus on the Holy Spirit within you and write down the following questions one after the other:

«Lord, what lie do I believe about you? »

«Lord, what is the origin of this lie? »

Say, «I decide to forgive the person (say his or her name) who is behind this lie. »

«Lord, what is the truth that you want me to believe? »

Then confess the truth that God is revealing to you.

Then ask him the question:

«Lord what have you got for me?»

If you don't understand the meaning of what God is saying or showing you, ask what it means. Repeat this process regularly and meditate on the truths you have received.

CHAPTER 11

PRAYING LIKE AN AMBASSADOR

Therefore, we are ambassadors for Christ, God making his appeal through us. We implore you on behalf of Christ, be reconciled to God.

(2 Corinthians 5:20)

A young man had asked me for an interview in my office; after having encouraged him, I ended praying for him. His eyes were closed and I could see that he was being touched by God. I waited for a few moments, but he stood still. Then I asked the Holy Spirit what I should do, and he invited me to wait. So I waited for fifteen minutes, and then the phone rang. I answered in another room, leaving the young man alone with the Lord. When I returned a few minutes later, I asked him what he had experienced. He told me that he had seen a great light and a figure dressed in white approaching him and talking to him. He added that he felt a great warmth on the right side of his body, like a radiation. Then he explained that Jesus had spoken to him and comforted him. I was amazed because it was the first time I had realized that supernatural activity was taking place while I was praying. As the months and years have passed since that day, I have discovered many ways that God wants to use us in prayer. I call this kind of prayer the Ambassador's Prayer. This is what I received from the Lord while preparing this chapter:

> *I have put my Spirit in you to guide you to destroy the works of the devil and establish my kingdom. When working with me, you will see my will being fulfilled. What is important is not what you can do, but what I will do when you will obey me by faith. Do not be afraid, I am with you.*

Establishing the Kingdom of God

God has put His Spirit in you to establish His kingdom through you. In the Second Epistle to the Corinthians, in chapter 5 verse 20, the apostle Paul writes that we serve as ambassadors for Christ. This is a very rich verse, so let's look at it together.

The function of ambassador is very important for a state. The ambassador is a spokesman for his government, he is sent to a foreign country with a mandate, an authority. The land of the embassy is considered a territory of the country it represents. Therefore, the laws and culture of that country prevail there. The ambassador's mission is also to promote the culture of his country to the host nation. Finally, an embassy can also become a place of refuge for an asylum seeker. If I enter the Embassy of France in Canada, I have access to resources and programs for French citizens even though I am thousands of kilometers away from my country. The Embassy of France in Canada is the government of France that is close to me.

As ambassadors for Christ, we are representatives of the kingdom of God for those we meet. But Jesus doesn't want you to just ride around in a nice diplomatic car with flags on the hood. No, we are ambassadors in office, called to action.

Heal the sick in it and say to them, The kingdom of God has come near to you.'

(Luke 10:9)

When Jesus gave this command to his disciples, he asked them to exercise the authority of the ambassador of the kingdom of heaven by healing the sick. We are therefore called to manifest the kingdom of God before proclaiming it. Announcing the kingdom of God should be explaining what people have just experienced through our prayer.

Destroy the works of the devil

The Lord has put His Spirit in you to guide you to destroy the works of the devil. Jesus Christ is the perfect model of the ambassador of the kingdom of heaven. All ambassadors of a country have direct communication with their government. They receive instructions, directives, and orders from their government. The reason I wanted to learn to hear God is to live what Jesus was living.

So Jesus said to them, "Truly, truly, I say to you, the Son can do nothing of his own accord, but only what he sees the Father doing. For whatever the Father does, that the Son does likewise.

(John 5.19)

The words that I speak to you I speak not of myself; and the Father that dwelleth in me, he doeth the works.

(John 14.10)

So Jesus did what he saw the Father do through visions and repeated the words he heard from his Father. This was the center of His ministry on earth. Jesus calls us to do the same and even greater works as He did. But to do what Jesus did, we must do it as He did, in total dependence and synchronicity with the Holy Spirit.

The more I listen to God and the more I obey Him by faith, the more fruit I see when I pray for people. Instead of praying for God to do what I want to do, I declare what he wants to do, and he does it!

how God anointed Jesus of Nazareth with the Holy Spirit and with power. He went about doing good and healing all who were oppressed by the devil, for God was with him.

(Acts of the Apostles 10:38)

One Sunday morning, my friend Matthew Gatet, who was visiting our church, received the following words during the prayer time before the meeting: «painful operations, severe pain, screws and bolts». He shared with me that he had received these words of knowledge. I then decided to share them with the congregation. We had already seen once before someone who had a knee prosthesis be free of pain and regain full mobility of his knee, to the astonishment of the doctor who had operated on him. So I knew that God could heal and wanted to perform a miracle that morning. Here is Pastor Jean-Marie Janvier's testimony:

I would like to share with you what Jesus did for me in April 2016. Following a work accident twenty-eight years ago, I had to undergo two major operations on my spine in order to immobilize the vertebrae with two metal rods screwed along my spine and to relieve the damaged discs. Unfortunately for me, the situation deteriorated more and more. The rods broke and I had to be operated a second time. In order to reduce the pain, I was given very powerful morphine medication for many years. Morphine, taken over a long period of time, creates an addiction in the subject that requires an increase in the daily doses taken, thus causing multiple long-term complications in the body. Thus, I had no choice but to agree to have an intrathecal pump installed (this is a pump installed under the skin with a catheter that sends the morphine directly into the spinal cord). In spite of this, the pain was continuous and the morphine only relieved me by about 40%. I slept between three and four hours a night. Most of the time, I could only sleep sitting on the edge of my bed, leaning forward to try to calm the pain. I was completely exhausted and the maximum dose of morphine I could take was reached. After twenty-eight long years of suffering, the Lord gave me grace by granting me my healing. That day, my wife and I had gone to join our daughter at the church she attends regularly, the Crossroads of the Nations. After an extraordinary time of praise, Pastor David made a call for healing, first for those who had chronic pain; second, those who could not be healed by medicine; and finally, those who had metal implants. At all these calls, I stood up, for this is what I was experiencing. Pastor David began to pray and asked all those who had stood up if they felt something in their bodies (heat, electric current, shivers), and if so, people were invited to come forward by raising their hands. Since I didn't feel anything at the time, I didn't raise my hands. Pastor David continued to pray, and it was then that I began to feel warmth in my back and got hotter and hotter. He again asked those who felt something to raise their hands, which I did with joy. Of six people, five sat down and I stood alone. Pastor David invited me to step forward and asked his team to surround me and pray for me. As they prayed, I felt my spine straighten and return to normal. Pastor David then asked me if I was still in pain, and it was then that I noticed that the pain in my lower back had completely disappeared. However, I was still feeling pain in the middle of my spine. They continued to pray and I had a vision. I saw angels repairing my vertebrae, but at the same time I saw demons trying to prevent this healing. I expressed what I saw to Pastor David who immediately asked a young woman to intercede. She did so without hesitation, supported in prayer by the congregation. The pain in the middle of my back disappeared completely. I was able to touch my feet in front of the congregation and bend my back and twist my body from side to side, which was impossible until then because of the metal bars screwed to my spine. Since that day, my life has completely changed. After my recovery, I consulted my specialist in order to decrease the dose of morphine I was taking daily. The doctor gradually decreased it until the morphine was replaced with salt water. Since that wonderful day, I have been walking confidently, without the need for a cane, my back has completely straightened up. I no longer need morphine to relieve my pain and I have more and more strength and energy to fulfill my destiny. My doctors try to understand, but find no conclusive answers to explain how after twenty-eight years of suffering, my pain has disappeared. The metal rods are still there, yet they are flexible as if I had none. I thank God for all His blessings to me and my family and I thank Pastor David Théry and his team for listening to and obeying the Holy Spirit.

In this testimony, notice that it is God who is at the origin of the prayer. Without the word of knowledge, we would not have prayed for this subject. Then the Holy Spirit encouraged us by manifesting His action with warmth in the body of Jean-Marie, which prompted us to persevere in prayer for 25 minutes until a complete healing. The Holy Spirit also showed us how to pray when giving Jean-Marie and a young woman on the prayer team the same vision. So we prayed according to the vision and blessed what God was doing. Jean-Marie's experience was miraculous, the metal rods along his spine are now flexible, which is medically impossible, but nothing is impossible for God!

When we understand our identity as ambassadors of God's kingdom and decide to serve in this role, God's kingdom is manifested in the lives of those we meet. The presence of the Holy Spirit in us has a purpose: to establish the kingdom of God, to do good to people, and to destroy the works of the devil.

Become a collaborator spectator of the Holy Spirit

By collaborating with the Holy Spirit, you will see His will being fulfilled. Many Christians are looking for a method to see the miraculous, but the method is simple, it is Jesus' method: you must collaborate with the Holy Spirit. To collaborate with the Holy Spirit is to be his mouth and hands. It is important to understand our role in this partnership. Our ignorance can block God's action. As I read the Bible carefully, I found that many of my prayers were not biblical. So I decided to pray as God asks and I got more results. I will now list some of my discoveries. Since these truths are biblical, you can apply them, too, no matter where you are.

The simplest form of prayer for someone is to bless them. But you still need to know how to bless someone. There is indeed a difference between asking God to bless a person and blessing that person.

> *The LORD spoke to Moses, saying, "Speak to Aaron and his sons, saying, Thus you shall bless the people of Israel: you shall say to them, The LORD bless you and keep you; the LORD make his face to shine upon you and be gracious to you; the LORD lift up his countenance upon you and give you peace" So shall they put my name upon the people of Israel, and I will bless them."*
>
> *(Numbers 6:22-27)*

In this text, God wants to bless the Israelites, it is his will, but he asks Aaron and his sons to collaborate with him. His ambassadors are instructed to follow his precise instructions. Do we, for our part, follow the Lord's guidance to see his kingdom manifest? Aaron was not to ask God to bless the people, he was to bless them himself, for that was the mandate he had received from the Lord. Aaron was to assume his authority. Only when he obeyed would God bless his people. This principle remains valid for us today. Before we pray for someone, we must know the Father's will. This will is contained in the Bible, but it can also be specifically revealed to us by the Holy Spirit. It is on the knowledge of God's will that we can pray with faith and believe that the Lord will act.

Therefore I tell you, whatever you ask in prayer, believe that you have received it, and it will be yours.

(Mark 11:24)

When I discovered this principle, I began to pray believing that my words trigger God's action. For example, instead of saying, «Lord, please bless Peter,» I now say, «Peter, I bless you in the name of Jesus. I now say, «Peter, I bless you in the name of Jesus,» and I expect the Holy Spirit to touch Peter. I often even ask at the end of my prayer if the person has experienced something, had a vision, heard God, because I expect this to happen. If I declare what God wants to do, He does it. So instead of praying everything that comes into my head, I begin with quietly asking the Lord how I should pray before I even open my mouth. Then I pray and declare what He shows me, speaking slowly, so that I can follow His directions as I receive them. It also allows the person to welcome the work of the Holy Spirit in them. Too often we think that God works only instantaneously. But this is not the case. For example, the peace of God may come very gradually and not be felt right away. We must therefore go at the pace of the Holy Spirit. What is important is not what I say, but what God does. Therefore my prayers are not meant to speak to the mind of the person I am praying for, but to initiate, accentuate and spotlight the work of the Holy Spirit in that person.

As you read these lines, you will surely feel helpless. How can you know what the Lord wants to do? This feeling of powerlessness combined with simple faith is the attitude of heart that allows God to use you. He knows that you can't do anything on your own, so He comes to the rescue of your infirmity.

For the law of the Spirit of life has set you free in Christ Jesus from the law of sin and death..

(Romans 8:2)

Remain dependent on the Holy Spirit and listen to Him whisper His guidance to you, then act as an ambassador and speak on behalf of your king.

No pressure, God wants to act through you.

What is important is not what you can do, but what God will do when you obey Him by faith. It is fundamental that you see your role as that of a trigger. Your prayer does not alter God's will, nor does it create the divine resources necessary for its fulfillment. God's will is expressed in his promises, and his fulfillment was realized when Jesus died on the cross and accomplished everything. Our role, as ambassadors, is to liberate what is available.

For all the promises of God find their Yes in him. That is why it is through him that we utter our Amen to God for his glory.

(2 Corinthians 1:20)

All of God's promises are yes in Jesus Christ. This means that spiritually they are already fulfilled. True faith is not satisfied with spiritual fulfillment, but triggers the materialization of that accomplishment.

Imagine that God's promises for Peter's life are contained in liquid form in a balloon suspended in the air above his head. The fact that this balloon is over his head represents God's will to bless him. The fact that it is filled represents the abundance of blessing available through the work of Jesus.

Blessed be the God and Father of our Lord Jesus Christ, who has blessed us in Christ with every spiritual blessing in the heavenly places.

(Ephesians 1:3)

What will allow the blessing to be released will be to pierce this balloon, to release the contents onto Peter. From a spiritual point of view, God grants us the revelation of His will for Peter through His Word and what the Holy Spirit communicates to us. But it is our prayer that releases the blessing. The «AMEN» we say to God in the name of Jesus is like an arrow that pierces the balloon and releases its contents. Amen means «so be it». It is not a request, it is a word of authority. When Jesus explained to the disciples how they should pray, he gave them this model:

Pray then like this: "Our Father in heaven, hallowed be your name. Your kingdom come, your will be done, on earth as it is in heaven.

(Matthew 6:9-10)

When we say, «Thy will be done,» we are collaborating with the Father to bring heaven down to earth. The wonderful thing about partnering with the Holy Spirit is that he often acts beyond what we can imagine.

During a call at the end of a meeting in the church of my friend Serge Herrbrech in Saint-Dié, I approached Vincent Kieffer, a 48-year-old man. I had never spoken to him before. I began to listen to the Holy Spirit to find out how to pray for him. The thought I received was that God wanted to communicate his fatherly love to him, especially because he had experienced violence from his father. Before I prayed, I asked him if his father had been abusive to him. He answered in the negative. (It is always good to humbly validate with the person what one believes one has received). I felt, however, that I had to take him in my arms so that he could experience the loving embrace of God the Father. I asked his permission, then hugged and embraced him and prayed that God's love would come and fill him. To my surprise, he collapsed to the ground with a newborn cry. He then received a first deposit of God's love. Six months later, while he was praying alone, he had a vision. He saw himself in his mother's womb, and he saw his father come close to the womb and cry out to him. He then felt a great emotional pain that left him after a few moments and was replaced by God's love. On that day Vincent realized that he had experienced an emotional shock in his mother's womb and that the Lord had just freed him from it. Since that day, he has been more open to the life of the Holy Spirit and fully enjoys God's love. God's will was to heal Vincent of a problem he did not know about. All that was needed was for an ambassador of God's kingdom to declare «AMEN! «in the name of Jesus, for God's will to be fulfilled.

Do not be afraid, God is with you.

Now Peter and John were going up to the temple at the hour of prayer, the ninth hour. And a man lame from birth was being carried, whom they laid daily at the gate of the temple that is called the Beautiful Gate to ask alms of those entering the temple. Seeing Peter and John about to go into the temple, he asked to receive alms. And Peter directed his gaze at him, as did John, and said, "Look at us." And he fixed his attention on them, expecting to receive something from them. But Peter said, "I have no silver and gold, but what I do have I give to you. In the name of Jesus Christ of Nazareth, rise up and walk!" And he took him by the right hand and raised him up, and immediately his feet and ankles were made strong.

(Acts of the Apostles 3.1-7).

Peter and John were in their daily life, they were on their way to prayer. God is often expected to act in church meetings, but the Holy Spirit is always in us. It is important to develop this awareness that He lives in you and that you have something to communicate to those you meet. As your awareness of God within you increases, your boldness and confidence to act as an ambassador will grow. I want to share with you now several ways to pray as an ambassador.

Pray a verse

You may receive a verse, a biblical reference, or the name of a biblical character. Do not underestimate the power of God's Word. A verse can be an answer to a specific prayer, it can trigger the action of the Holy Spirit, or can become a promise, a confirmation for the person receiving it. Remember that the Bible is the sword of the Spirit. So as you declare this verse, do it with faith and authority as if you had a sword in your hand and were cutting a rope. When a knight was raised by his king, the king would place his sword on his shoulders to make the new status official. When you declare the Word of God about someone according to the guidance of the Holy Spirit, it is the king of kings who acts through you to bless the person, it is a trigger of God's favor and blessing for him.

If you pray according to the Bible, you are sure to remain biblical! For less charismatic people, this makes it easier to receive the content of the prayer, because it is biblical. To develop this way of praying, it is important to feed yourself abundantly on the Bible so that the Word of God may dwell in you in all its richness (Col 3:16).

For example, if you are praying for someone and you think about the story of David and Goliath, you can pray that the person will have David's boldness in the face of the giants in his life, and that God will give him courage and strength. If you are with someone who is tired or downcast, you can pray for God's rain to run down on them and refresh them, as in Psalm 68.

Rain in abundance, O God, you shed abroad; you restored your inheritance as it languished.

(Psalms 68.9)

There are no limits to what God can do through His Word.

See what God does

It is possible that God is showing you an image that announces what He wants to do. In this case, you can simply share what you have seen and declare it. For example, if you see a plant blooming, you can say, «I pray for the blooming, the blossoming in your life, in the name of Jesus. »

Being a channel of blessing

It can also happen that you have an animated vision in which God reveals to you what He is doing.

One day, Sylvie shared with me that her hip was hurting very badly. I sat beside her and put my hand on her and asked the Holy Spirit how to pray. Then I saw a waterfall of flowing water. I continued to lay my hand on Sylvie without saying anything. After a few moments, I asked her how she felt. She answered that the pain had greatly diminished. I listened to the Holy Spirit again and saw the waterfall again. I waited without saying anything while I watched the waterfall flow, and then the waterfall disappeared from my mind. Then I asked my wife if there was any pain left; there was none left.

And these signs will accompany those who believe: in my name they will cast out demons; they will speak in new tongues; they will pick up serpents with their hands; and if they drink any deadly poison, it will not hurt them; they will lay their hands on the sick, and they will recover."

(Mark 16:17-18)

Jesus did not specify that it was necessary to say words with the laying on of hands. If I focus on the Holy Spirit, I will become a channel between the reality of heaven and the person's need. I regularly pray without words for people and they are touched by the Holy Spirit. You can do it too!

Undo the enemy's work

The Holy Spirit reveals not only what God does, but also the work of the enemy. It is therefore possible to see something negative. This is then exercising the gift of discernment the spirits. For example, you may see a black whirlwind over someone or an arrow stuck in their back. This does not mean that this is God's plan. On the contrary, the Holy Spirit reveals the enemy's work to you so that you may cancel it. This is what Elisha experienced when he heard the plans of the king of Syria and was able to warn the king of Israel so that he would not be ambushed.

> *Once when the king of Syria was warring against Israel, he took counsel with his servants, saying, "At such and such a place shall be my camp." But the man of God sent word to the king of Israel, "Beware that you do not pass this place, for the Syrians are going down there." And the king of Israel sent to the place about which the man of God told him. Thus he used to warn him, so that he saved himself there more than once or twice. And the mind of the king of Syria was greatly troubled because of this thing, and he called his servants and said to them, "Will you not show me who of us is for the king of Israel?" And one of his servants said, "None, my lord, O king; but Elisha, the prophet who is in Israel, tells the king of Israel the words that you speak in your bedroom." And he said, "Go and see where he is, that I may send and seize him." It was told him, "Behold, he is in Dothan."*
>
> *(2 Kings 6.8-13)*

Therefore, do not make the mistake of agreeing with what the enemy wants to do, of thinking that it is a imminent, or that it is God's will. On the contrary, pray to cancel the enemy's plan and declare God's blessing. Ask the Holy Spirit how to undo the enemy's work and simply do it in the name of Jesus.

To take the example of the arrow, it must be removed in the name of Jesus and returned to where it came from. If you have seen darkness, call the light of God. To give a simple piece of advice, simply state the opposite of what the enemy wanted to do.

The Holy Spirit can reveal the emotions of the person you are praying for.

Validate with the person (ask them how they feel) and then state the opposite if their emotions were negative. For example, if you feel their anxiety, release peace and security. If you feel their sadness, call on them God's joy, an oil of joy, a garment of praise. Do not insist if the person does not confirm what you felt. You may be wrong, or they may not dare to tell you how they feel, or the Holy Spirit may want to solve a problem they are not aware of. Declaring God's joy or peace will not hurt anyone.

Make a prophetic gesture

The expression «prophetic act» may seem intimidating, but it is simply making a gesture that symbolizes an action of God. For example: taking off a weight, pouring the oil of joy, washing feet, hugging, etc.

When inspired by the Holy Spirit (that's the meaning of the prophetic word here), our actions trigger God's action. You will find many prophetic gestures in the Bible; I leave you to discover them for yourself. Just think of Moses raising his hands in battle (Exodus 17:11), Joshua turning and shouting around Jericho (Joshua 6:20), or Gideon breaking a jug (Judges 7:19-22). In the New Testament, we can cite the case where Jesus makes mud with his saliva to heal the blind man (John 9).

For example, one can pray for a garment of praise over a person and make a hand gesture to surround him or her as if one had a real garment to cover them with.

Declare a word or a short sentence

A Roman soldier came to Jesus and said to him: Therefore I did not presume to come to you. But say the word, and let my servant be healed.

(Luke 7.7)

A word from Jesus is enough. As ambassadors of Christ, it is up to us to say that word now, but we can only repeat what we hear from the Holy Spirit.

Therefore, as you listen to the Holy Spirit, a simple word or phrase may be communicated to you in a quietly or in a persistent manner. After analyzing the biblical basis for this prayer, simply declare it in the name of Jesus. For example: «Speed up,» «It's over! «or, «Case closed,» or «More! ». This may sound simplistic, but if that's what God says, that's enough!

Collaborating with the action of the Holy Spirit

The Holy Spirit works in time. I often compare our collaboration with him to lighting a wood fire. When I was younger, I was a scout for a few years. The thing I liked best was to light the fire, especially in the morning, when it was a matter of rekindling the tiny embers left over from the previous day's fire. I remember several times having my eyebrows singed from blowing on the embers. When we pray according to the guidance of the Holy Spirit, a spark is lit, but it is easily missed, as it is imperceptible at first. It is faith in God's work accompanied by spiritual sensitivity that will allow us to continue «blowing» on the embers until the fire can no longer be extinguished. When you pray, focus on the Holy Spirit within you. You can begin to feel the anointing flow through you and learn to accompany what God is doing. For example, you can pray like this: «Lord, I bless what you are doing, (silence and listening to God) thank you lord (silence and listening to God) more Lord ! (silence and listening to God).

This is not the time to get agitated and pray for everything that comes into your head, to recite all the Bible verses you have memorized, or to think about what you are going to do next. If you concentrate, you allow the person to receive more. At a certain point, you will feel that you have done what you had to do and you can leave the person with the Holy Spirit. The Holy Spirit may also be able to tell you that He is talking to the person or giving the person a vision. So ask God to increase your spiritual sensitivity.

> *And Elijah said to Ahab, "Go up, eat and drink, for there is a sound of the rushing of rain." So Ahab went up to eat and to drink. And Elijah went up to the top of Mount Carmel. And he bowed himself down on the earth and put his face between his knees. And he said to his servant, "Go up now, look toward the sea." And he went up and looked and said, "There is nothing." And he said, "Go again," seven times. And at the seventh time he said, "Behold, a little cloud like a man's hand is rising from the sea." And he said, "Go up, say to Ahab, 'Prepare your chariot and go down, lest the rain stop you.'" And in a little while the heavens grew black with clouds and wind, and there was a great rain. And Ahab rode and went to Jezreel.*
>
> *(1 Kings 18.41-45)*

When Elijah prayed for rain to return to Israel, he heard the sound of rain before a single cloud was visible in the sky.

This rumbling was a supernatural indication of God's will. So Elijah collaborated with the Lord when praying the same prayer seven times with perseverance. Once he saw the little cloud, he stopped praying, for nothing could stop the rain anymore. If you receive an indication from the Holy Spirit, collaborate with him and persist in faith that heaven will come down in a person's life.

This type of prayer is especially appropriate for communicating peace, joy, love of God, courage, boldness, for the baptism in the Holy Spirit, or for consolation.

After praying, ask the person for whom you prayed what he or she experienced, felt or saw. First, because it is a demonstration of your faith. We expect prayer to be effective. Second, because if you don't ask the question, chances are that the person will not share it with you. Often people are afraid to express what they have experienced because they fear not being believed or judged, they are analyzing their experience and may be surprised at what they are going through. If you ask the question, you will hear what God is doing when you pray and your faith will increase, which will give you more confidence the next time.

This list of the Ambassador's prayers is of course not exhaustive and you, too, will discover new ways the Lord will use you.

I suggest you pray with me:

Thank you, Lord, because you put your Holy Spirit in me and made me an ambassador for Christ.

I ask your forgiveness for my lack of cooperation with the Holy Spirit. I put my mouth and my hands and feet at your disposal to trigger your action in the name of Jesus.

May the Amen that comes out of my mouth, led by Your Spirit, materialize the blessings that Jesus won on the cross.

Holy Spirit, guide me to establish the kingdom of God around me.

In the name of Jesus, Amen

I want to pray for you now that you will receive, like Jesus, this anointing of the Holy Spirit and power. Read the following prayer and then take a few minutes of silence before God to let Him work in you.

Come Holy Spirit, let your anointing and power be poured out now upon your child.

Equip him/her with your authority, faith and boldness to serve as an ambassador for Christ. In the name of Jesus, instruct him/her, guide him/her to do the works you have prepared beforehand for him/her.

May the works of the devil be destroyed in his or her path. Make him/her more aware of your presence in him/her, in the name of Jesus.

Let him/her become a channel to bring heaven down to earth. Holy Spirit, put on your child as a glove, do your will through him/her. In the name of Jesus, Amen.

Now take action and go pray for people around you!

CHAPTER 12

BECOMING A SOURCE OF ENCOURAGEMENT

But Moses said to him, "Are you jealous for my sake? Would that all the LORD'S people were prophets, that the LORD would put his Spirit on them!"

(Numbers 11.29)

Moses made this prayer after God rested His Spirit on 70 elders of the people to prophesy too. Moses realized the value of prophecy to the people. What he prayed for and desired something, the Holy Spirit made it possible. When writing the last chapter of this book, I want to conclude with you about the study of the first text we discussed in chapter one.

On the last day of the feast, the great day, Jesus stood up and cried out, "If anyone thirsts, let him come to me and drink. Whoever believes in me, as the Scripture has said, Out of his heart will flow rivers of living water.'" Now this he said about the Spirit, whom those who believed in him were to receive, for as yet the Spirit had not been given, because Jesus was not yet glorified.

(John 7.37-39)

Jesus not only said that there was a spring in you, but that rivers of living water would flow from you. God's plan is to make you a walking spring. This is what I have received from the Lord while preparing this chapter:

The source that I have put in you must spring up and flow on those around you so that they may taste my love, so that my life may pass through you. My words through you will produce life in hearts, give courage to my children. Go forth humbly by faith and observe the fruit.

The source that God has put in you must spring up and flow on those around you.

Not only can you pray for people as an ambassador to establish the kingdom of God in their lives, but more than that, you can give them words of life, encouragement, consolation. Jesus said that his words were spirit and life and that he was not speaking on his own authority, but that he was repeating what he heard the Father say. As you learn to hear the voice of God, the Lord will begin to speak to you for those around you.

This source of love that you draw from does not spring up only for you, but must spill over to those you meet. The peace, security, and comfort you experience in listening to God will also be perceived by those to whom you prophesy. Are you willing to make yourself available to water those around you with God's love?

We may have mysterious conceptions about prophecy, but here is a simple definition: to prophesy is to hear God's voice for someone and to share with them what one has received.

In the New Testament, prophecy is defined by the apostle Paul :

On the other hand, the one who prophesies speaks to people for their upbuilding and encouragement and consolation.
(1 Corinthians 14:3)

A modern translation of the French Bible translates it this way:

But he who transmits divine messages speaks to others to advance them in faith, to encourage them and to console them.
(1 Corinthians 14:3)

There are many levels of prophecy, but all God's children can prophesy on the first level, that is, encourage, build faith and comfort from God. You have certainly noticed that when listening to the Lord, you receive encouragement and comfort and your faith increases.

Everyone needs to be encouraged, inspired and consoled on a regular basis. God is encouraging. Without his encouragement, how can we walk by faith? I believe that many unfaithful Christians would have persevered in their walk with God if they had had more encouragement. I am not talking about flattery or human words of limited scope and fleeting impact, but words of life that come from the heart of God. God's words are creative and produce life in the heart of the one who receives them. The Lord seeks messengers to communicate encouragement to His children. He wants to use you to prophesy in the lives of those around you. You can become a source of consolation, faith and courage.

For you can all prophesy one by one, so that all may learn and all be encouraged.

(1 Corinthians 14:31)

Yes, you, too, can prophesy, that is, encourage, inspire, and console from God. It is often thought that prophets are special people, and to a certain extent it is true, because they experience special things with the Lord. But the role of prophets is to train believers in the exercise of prophecy. This is why Paul says that all can prophesy.

One of the famous prophets of the Bible is Isaiah. Beyond divine visions (Isaiah 6), messianic messages (Isaiah 7:53), eschatological messages (concerning the end times or the future: Isaiah 11:6 and continuing), messages for the nation of Israel (Isaiah 41) and for the surrounding nations (Isaiah 11:13), Isaiah also prophesied on an individual level, as Paul invites us to do. We have no record of these individual prophecies, but we see below how God used the prophet:

The Lord GOD has given me the tongue of those who are taught, that I may know how to sustain with a word him who is weary. Morning by morning he awakens; he awakens my ear to hear as those who are taught. The Lord GOD has opened my ear, and I was not rebellious; I turned not backward.

(Isaiah 50:4-5)

The Lord is the one who opened Isaiah's ear every morning to hear from Him. Just as a letter carrier receives mail to be delivered daily, so you can receive daily prophetic words for those you will meet, whether you know them or not. God shared messages with Isaiah, and Isaiah was the mailman. The reason for these deposits was that Isaiah had agreed to be God's messenger.

And I heard the voice of the Lord saying, "Whom shall I send, and who will go for us?" Then I said, "Here I am! Send me."

(Isaiah 6.8)

This invitation was not just for a stroll or a walk for Jesus. God was looking for a spokesperson, someone who would speak for him to his people. That's why the French modern Bible makes this invitation like this:

Then I heard the Lord ask, «Whom shall I send? Who will be our spokesman? I said, «I am, and you can send me.

(Isaiah 6:8, Modern French Bible)

This invitation from God is still with us today. Will you answer it? Will you make yourself available so that the people around you may be encouraged and comforted by the words that the Lord has for them? You too can experience it by being ready and listening to the Holy Spirit. He will instruct you.

The Lord GOD has given me the tongue of those who are taught, that I may know how to sustain with a word him who is weary. Morning by morning he awakens; he awakens my ear to hear as those who are taught.

(Isaiah 50:4)

Always remember that Isaiah had to learn, be instructed and trained by God to prophesy. It is an apprenticeship, a daily relearning, because each person is different and God will speak to them in a personalized way. There is no routine with the Lord. It is therefore necessary to have a teachable attitude, an attitude of disciple, one of apprenticeship. But remember that your ability comes from God, not from your experience. It is He who gives the words, the language, draws your attention and makes you listen, as translated from the Sower's version. Stay tuned, then go and communicate what you have received.

The words of God through you will produce life in hearts.

When consulting the different French versions, I measured the impact of Isaiah's words on the hearts of the recipients. André Chouraqui translates «to sustain with a word» by «to revive with a word». This makes me think of the Roman centurion of the Gospels who said to Jesus: «Say just one word and my servant will be healed. «A prophetic word can be enough to give life to what was dying. Some of your fellow brothers and sisters in Christ are like in a spiritual intensive care. The word of God that you will bring them has the power to revive them, like a cardiac defibrillator. That is the power of God's creative word. It can also be translated as «to lift up discouraged hearts» (Zadoc), «to bring comfort» (Jerusalem Bible), «to encourage» (Word of Life Bible), «to sustain» (Darby), «to strengthen» (Sower's Bible), «to relieve the weak» (TOB). The prophetic word is not just information, but it has a direct effect on the heart of the person receiving it. It produces the same life in the recipient as when God speaks to you personally.

Isaiah gave prophetic words to kings and nations, but also to his contemporaries. Here is the condition of those to whom Isaiah prophesied: «the weary one» (Darby), «the exhausted one» (New Bible, Second Edition), «the weak one» (Modern

French Bible Edition), «the weary one» (Chouraqui), «the downhearted one» (Second, New Geneva Edition), «the weak one» (Word of Life Bible). Many people around you are in this state. For some, it is obvious. For others, the suffering is hidden behind a fake smile. They desperately need encouragement. The Lord wants to use you to communicate words from Him to them. Will you accept this mission? Many give in to the harassment of the devil, lacking the strength to resist him and drive him away. If you accept to become a source of encouragement, you will be like a survival ration for a soldier on the front line: a source of strength to persevere in the fight of faith.

Walk in faith and observe the fruit.

The Lord GOD has opened my ear, and I was not rebellious; I turned not backward.

(Isaiah 50:5)

Right after explaining how God communicates prophetic messages to him for his contemporaries, Isaiah mentions that he does not rebel, nor does not back down. These expressions speak to us first of all of availability and obedience, but more than that.

Isaiah mentions the rebellion. We can think of the prophet Jonah who rebelled because he did not want to share God's message to the people of Nineveh. But why would Isaiah want to rebel and refuse to encourage someone who is tired? The reason is that God sees people in a different way than we do. We need to remember that we are not the authors of the prophecy, just the messengers. So we must trust God and do not rely on our own reasoning. We prophesy by faith. We tend to crush the one who is on the ground when the Lord wants to lift him up. We do not know the suffering in our hearts, but God hears the voice of tears. That is why He may ask you to communicate a message of consolation to someone who seems joyful. We are naturally inclined to judge people's behavior as the Lord sees the deep motivations and aspirations of our hearts.

From now on, therefore, we regard no one according to the flesh. Even though we once regarded Christ according to the flesh, we regard him thus no longer.

(2 Corinthians 5:16)

That is why God may ask you to call out someone whose conduct seems to be in opposition to Him. In such situations, we should act by faith and not rely on what we see or think. What the Lord expects of you is that you stop talking to people from your own perceptions, but from His perspective. You can only prophesy by faith. This is what Paul will tell the Romans:

Having gifts that differ according to the grace given to us, let us use them: if prophecy, in proportion to our faith.

(Romans 12.6)

Prophesying by faith is risky, because it is possible to make mistakes, to lose our reputation, that is why we can be tempted to rebel, to resist and not share what God tells us for someone.

You will not measure the impact of the prophecy when receiving it, for you are not the recipient. Remember, you are like a letter carrier. It is the sender and the content of the letter that is important, not the experience of the letter carrier. But without letter carriers, there is no mail delivery. When the post office goes on strike, it disrupts an entire country. Likewise, the Church suffers because there are too few Christians who prophesy.

I suggest you write a letter from God to someone. Begin by asking the Lord to whom you should write. Then ask him what he wants to say to the person. Simply write it and after you have examined what you have received, hand the letter over. Just as you can build on what you receive from God when writing what you have received, the recipient will be able to read the letter again, examine it, remember what is good and be encouraged.

Only the love we have for others will allow us to take the risk of speaking on behalf of God. When we love someone, we are ready to do anything for their good.

Give a taste of God's love

Love must be the motivation and fruit of prophecy. We have just seen that the Lord is the source of encouragement, that His words are powerful to lift up hearts and that it is through faith that we can be effective. Why, then, are there so few prophetic words shared among God's people? Why do so few Christians communicate God's messages to those who do not yet know him?

For people to experience the Father's love when you prophesy, it is important to remember the purpose of prophecy: to encourage, comfort, and build faith. To summarize even more simply, people must feel loved by God when you prophesy, for God is love. The Apostle Paul inserted a full chapter on the importance of love in the exercise of spiritual gifts between chapters 12 and 14 describing them (see First Corinthians). This famous passage on the definition of love is not only a description of what love between humans should look like, but it also depicts God's love for us. Here is another way to read this text:

> *Love is patient and kind; love does not envy or boast; it is not arrogant or rude. It does not insist on its own way; it is not irritable or resentful; it does not rejoice at wrongdoing, but rejoices with the truth. Love bears all things, believes all things, hopes all things, endures all things.*
>
> *(1 Corinthians 13:4-7)*

So before you communicate prophetic words to someone, in addition to putting them through the same tests as when you listen to God for yourself (Is this biblical? Does this sound like the nature of God? Did I have my eyes fixed on Jesus? Is it spontaneous?), you must give them the test of love.

Since you are not the recipient of the message, you will not be able to evaluate its effect in the person's heart BEFORE you share it with them. That said, you MUST ask yourself the following questions:

- ·Would I feel loved by God by receiving this word myself?
- ·Is this encouraging?
- ·Would this bring me closer to God?
- ·Would that comfort me?
- ·Does this manifest God's gentleness?

- ·Does this reflect God's goodness?
- ·Does this testify to God's patience?
- ·Does this express God's grace?
- ·Does it communicate hope?

Of course, it is possible that what you receive may not meet all these criteria, but you must discard any negative word, any accusation, anything that is not biblical or that would be demeaning or discouraging, anything that would be condemning, despicable, hopeless or that would distance the person from God. When God speaks to us, he draws us closer to us and draws us to himself.

The Lord invites you to observe the fruit of what you will share in people's lives. The fruit of prophecy must be the perception of God's love by the one who receives it. You will see the impact when you speak with the person to whom the Lord had given you a message for.

Walk humbly

Prophecy does not have a definite form, it does not need to begin with «Thus said the Lord» or end with speaking in tongues. You do not need to be in church to prophesy. You can simply say, «I was praying for you and practicing listening to God, this is what I believe I received for you ... Does this mean something to you? »

In fact, it is even possible to prophesy without saying so. This is very useful especially with non-Christians. In the same way that you can say to someone: «Courage, you are not alone, I am with you! «to give them comfort, you can share a

God-inspired word with supernatural impact. The difference is the source. A human word will have limited impact, but a word from the Lord will revive the heart of the one who hears it. The person watered by this word will have a concrete taste of God's love. This may then allow you to pray for him or her, or to continue the conversation.

I was driving with Sylvie and we were coming back from a regional youth meeting. In the back of the car, two young Christian women were on the road with us. As I was talking with Sylvie, I was seized by the Holy Spirit, so I looked in the rear-view mirror and called out to one of the young women behind me: «Listen carefully to what I'm going to tell you, Aline, when God has said something, he doesn't change his mind, you can rely on his word. Have you understood? God does not change his mind. »

A year later, Aline got engaged. She came to see me and reminded me of that word that I had completely forgotten. The young woman told me that night she was questioning what God had told her about her future husband. She wondered if the Lord had changed His mind under the circumstances, because she was not yet seeing the fulfillment of what He had promised her. It was then that I had spoken this word to her without realizing its significance. Aline later married and started a beautiful family with her husband.

Life by faith is based on prophecy; everyone needs encouragement to continue God's plan. Let the spring that flows within you spring forth! I invite you to pray with me now.

Thank you Holy Spirit for the fountain of living water that you are in me. I decide to let it gush around me to bless your children. Here I am, use me. Make me your spokesperson, may your love enliven me, push me and shine through my words. Holy Spirit, open my ears so that I may receive the words of encouragement that your children need to hear. I choose to take the risk of opening my mouth. In the name of Jesus, Amen.

I will now pray for you. Read the following prayer and then take a few minutes of silence before God to let Him work in you.

Thank you Father for your child who listens to you, I now bless him/her in the name of Jesus. Make him/her a source of encouragement, consolation and strength. I pray that the gift of prophecy will be activated and multiplied in his/her life in the name of Jesus. Protect his or her faith as a child and allow him or her to see the fruit of his or her obedience. I pray that he/she may prophesy in the midst of your children, but also to those who do not yet know you. May your Word be in him/her like a fire that he/she cannot contain, like a hammer that breaks the rock and like a refreshing rain that sustains weary hearts. Let his cup overflow, astonish him/her for your glory. In the name of Jesus, Amen.

Practice exercise

Now it's time to put into practice what you've just read! I suggest that you write a letter from God to someone you know. Choose a person and write his or her name, then listen to God and ask this question:

«Lord, what do you want to say to him? »

Play instrumental music, e.g. by clicking on the following address:

entdi.eu/piano

Then write down what you receive, then examine it and humbly share what you have received. Then ask him/her what he/she thinks about it. You can write the testimony in your journal.

Did you like the content of this book?

Offer one to a friend so that you may listen to God together, progress is faster with a partner. I also encourage you to bless your pastor and give him a copy.

Have you had any experiences with God as a result of reading this book? Please send me your testimonies to the following address: contact@ecolemsf.com

Check my website davidthery.com to discover my other books !

Did you like the drawings in the book? I recommend the books of Alain Auderset. Discover Alain's ministry on his website:

Auderset.com

Date in the forest 1 and 2 will be an inspiration in your walk to listen to God.